3 1160 00249 1061

D1597842

BLOOMFIELD TOWNSHIP PUBLIC LIBRARY
BLOOMFIELD HILLS, MICHIGAN 48013

The Language of Flowers

Laura Peroni

Illustrations by Marilena Pistoia

Crown Publishers, Inc.
New York

The quotation on page 122 is taken from *Swann's Way* by Marcel Proust, translated by C. K. Scott Moncrieff (Random House, New York, 1964) and is reproduced by kind permission of Random House, Inc.

Appendix by Paola Violani

Copyright © 1984 Arnoldo Mondadori Editore S.p.A., Milan
English translation copyright © 1985 Arnoldo Mondadori
Editore S.p.A., Milan
Translated by Sylvia Mulcahy

All rights reserved. No part of this book may be reproduced or transmitted in any form or by any means, electronic or mechanical, including photocopying, recording, or by any information storage and retrieval system, without permission in writing from the publisher.

Originally published in 1984 in Italy by Arnoldo Mondadori Editore S.p.A., Milan under the title Il Linguaggio dei Fiori.

Published in the United States in 1985 by Crown Publishers, Inc., One Park Avenue, New York, New York 10016 and simultaneously in Canada by General Publishing Company Limited.

CROWN is a trademark of Crown Publishers, Inc.

Printed in Italy

Library of Congress Cataloging in Publication Data

Peroni, Laura
     The language of flowers.

     1. Flower language.   2. Flowers in art.
I. Pistoia, Marilena.   II. Title.
GR780.P46   1985   001.56   85-11688
ISBN 0-517-55802-5

First American edition

10   9   8   7   6   5   4   3   2   1

Contents

MAR - 7 1988 & TAYLO

Thou shalt, at one glance behold
The daisy and the marigold,
White plumed lilies, and the first
Hedge-grown primrose that hath
burst;/Shaded hyacinth, alway
Sapphire queen of the mid-May
And every leaf and every flower.

John Keats, *Ode to Fancy*

Foreword

I must confess to a scant knowledge concerning flowers and the way they live – I restrict myself merely to contemplating them. Once on a journey to Milan, a near neighbour of mine, Professor Henry Robert Cocker, who is an eminent international botanist and thus knows infinitely more about flowers than I do, held me spellbound for three hours by expounding on a single botanical topic – the miracle of reproduction. However, in those three hours the word "miracle" was never mentioned and this created a great, inexplicable and warm friendship between Professor Cocker and me. We talked non-stop about sex, without once using the word, through the metaphor of flowers.

I am often fascinated by flowers, especially by poppies and it was because of them that I began to read Laura Peroni's lovely book. Its charm lies in the fact that each piece of text is a complementary essay to the wonderful illustrations by Marilena Pistoia, which depict the flowers in their smallest detail. The notes that accompany the illustrations contain interesting facts and stories about the flowers taken from literature and folklore. The history and legends associated with the poppy, for example, go back through the millennia. These notes are rather like fables and it is not difficult to lose oneself in an opiate dream (pour cause) *as though drifting through oriental gardens. And how evocative, too, are the notes on the tulip, a word that stems from "turban." In a few words, a splendid scene is projected of processions of ambling tortoises bearing lighted lanterns during harem festivities. Many of the other myths and legends throughout the book are equally splendid. There is a history or an anecdote for every flower. And all is related with such brevity and lightness of tone that the flowers are really made to bloom before us.*

I have already said that I always restrict myself merely to contemplating flowers. Such contemplation is never abstract, as is so often thought, but like everything else, is very real indeed. The reality we face as we contemplate – and reflect on – the flowers we see in spring, summer and autumn in the countryside, is none other than youth, love and death – in other words, the brevity of life's span. In gazing at those great patches of crimson, like bloodstains in the cornfields, we draw nearer to look more closely. Each poppy stands in all its splendid, silky, ephemeral delicacy, an emblem of lightness and youth. Its brief life reminds us how fragile, short and delicate our own life may be. By this I mean our life on earth in the fullest sense, when our sensitivities are at their height. These are the kind of reflections, which give comfort in the contemplation of beauty and the realization of nature's wastefulness in allowing an infinite number of seeds to die or remain sterile in order that one poppy – or a field of poppies – might survive. In another way, however, such thoughts can sadden us as we are made to face the fact that the brevity of a poppy's life – and of thousands of other flowers – is a measure of the brevity of our own life and of the brevity of everything. A sad reflection.

Let us also consider beauty for its own sake, the philosophy of the beautiful, in a word, aesthetics, and aestheticism. Aesthetics embraces the concept and practice of enjoying, understanding and absorbing beauty. Aestheticism, on the other hand, is usually taken to mean not only an appreciation of beauty but an exaggerated dependence on it. The Romantics were acutely aware of beauty for some of them died in their search for it. There are some people – as there are some flowers – whose beauty is such that to contemplate it may inspire love but also lead to obsession. Such an emotion can be pleasurable and enable us to enjoy life by means of looking at things around us in a reflective way so that we can identify with the stem, the corolla and the seeds of a poppy, with its colour and with its brevity of life; and then, perhaps, one might comtemplate the life of a tree, and then of a person and then of literary, poetic, musical and pictorial works of art. And so, going from one identification to another, from one obsession to another, life will be lived.

In her delightful accompanying text Laura Peroni is, in fact, saying all this; she tells us, though, not like a poet-botanist but rather as a botanist-poet. The greatest of the Japanese haiku *poets, Basho, was also a botanist – the most beautiful flower of Japanese poetry but, unlike the flowers we know, he is immortal.*

Goffredo Parise

The Flowers

Acacia and Mimosa (Sensitive Plant)

The yellow flowers of acacias (also known as wattles in Australia where many kinds are native) and the pink flowers of the smaller, true mimosa or sensitive plant are very alike in appearance and do, in fact, belong to the same family, the *Leguminosae*. (Mimosa is also an old common name for the acacias.)

In past centuries, the qualities of purity, chaste love and sensitivity were associated with both the acacia and the mimosa. The following lines written in the late eighteenth century by Erasmus Darwin, grandfather of the famous Charles Darwin, reflect these sentiments:

Weak with nice sense the chaste Mimosa stands,
From each rude touch withdraws her timid hands;
Oft as light clouds o'erpass the summerglade,
Alarm'd she trembles at the moving shade.

The Victorian era undoubtedly produced some of the most serious and imaginative interpreters of the language of flowers and during this period, the acacia was widely regarded as a symbol of platonic love, a conception that greatly appealed to the Victorian outlook. However, traditions change with the times and it is rare to find such an association today. Instead, the fluffy yellow flowers have become identified with the feminist movement in some countries as symbols of freedom and autonomy. The femine quality of acacia is emphasized in many countries, too, by the traditional giving of sprays of the spring-flowering kinds to women on March 8 or thereabouts to celebrate Women's Day.

Acacia and Mimosa
(Sensitive Plant)

Acacia

It was the custom in England during the nineteenth century for those girls who were less than pretty to wear a spray of acacia in a jacket buttonhole or in their hair. Sometimes they would go further and wear a blouse or carry a kerchief embroidered with the yellow flowers. In each case, the meaning was the same – to make the world aware of their high-minded ideological superiority.

Some American Indians, however, give a very different meaning to those yellow flowers. While their customary festivals are in progress, when traditions and ceremonials abound, a promise of love is conveyed by a ritual gesture in which every young man who has serious intentions gives a spray of acacia to the girl who has set his heart on fire.

The 800 or so *Acacia* species, whose flowers are mostly sweetly fragrant, grow wild in the temperate areas of Africa and Asia as well as in the tropical regions of Australia and America. However, conditions in the Mediterranean areas of Europe suit them very well; they also flourish around the lakes of northern Italy where the temperature range is not too extreme. Cold weather and frost will damage an acacia tree to the extent that the more exposed branches will die but, the next year, new shoots will appear from the more healthy joints, near the trunk. In very cold regions, the plants are grown in greenhouses.

Young, tender acacia flowers, either singly or in sprays, can be dipped in batter to make into fritters. The flowers of certain species are the source of gum arabic.

Acacia

Acanthus

In A.D. 50 Pliny the Elder suggested in one of his treatises on botany that the elegant acanthus (also known as bear's-breech) would be ideal for planting around the confines of Roman gardens.
A hundred years before, Virgil had imagined that much contested and fascinating woman, Helen of Troy, draped in a white peplum with edges decorated with acanthus and beech leaves.
But it was an Athenian sculptor, Callimachus, who, in 500 B.C., was one of the first to notice the beautiful shape of the acanthus. This outstanding sculptor-architect was particularly well known for his inlaid work; his skill in working on marble with a chisel was undeniable and he was able to shape the soft folds of fabric and the precise, delicate lines of figures and faces. Supporters of the strict classical tradition, however, regarded his work as decadent.
It is said that, as Callimachus was walking in the outskirts of his city one bright spring morning, he came upon the tomb of a lovely young girl who had died tragically on the eve of her wedding. As he stood meditating by the grave, he noticed a white veil, caught by some nearby plants, billowing gently in the breeze. Underneath it was a large stone basket brimming with trinkets, ornaments and flowers, which a plant growing nearby had enveloped to the brim with its dark green leaves. The sculptor returned to his studio and began to draw the whole composition created by the basket and acanthus plant, which had inspired him so greatly. He had, in fact, conceived that most elaborate piece of classical architecture, the Corinthian capital. The acanthus is part of the landscape in nearly all Mediterranean regions. It is a vigorous grower, its outside leaves bent like bows while the central ones stand tall and austere, acting as a corona around the greenish-white, pink or purple-lilac flowers. The plant grows mainly on the banks of the Nile, in the cooler hills around Athens, the Roman countryside and in Spain.
Acanthus leaves were used as patterns by numerous craftsmen to decorate ceramics of all kinds and for the furniture of the ancient Romans, especially during the latter part of the Roman Empire. The motif was also a feature of the Empire Style, which came into fashion at the court of Napoleon. Percier and Fontaine, who were engaged to furnish and decorate Malmaison, Versailles, the Louvre, Fontainebleau, the Elysée and even the throneroom in the Tuileries Palace, included the acanthus leaf with the Bacchus figures, gorgons, chimeras, sphinxes and caryatids, eagles and snakes that were typical decorations on so many furnishings of that period.

Acanthus

Aconite

In their arrangement of spikes along a central stem, aconite flowers resemble a squad of ancient helmeted warriors. Their decidedly strange appearance, and the fact that the entire plant is poisonous, has given rise over the centuries to many myths and legends, in all of which the aconite is depicted as the flower of revenge and wrongful love. We can only surmise that it was used by some of our more cruel and jealous ancestors as a fatal weapon against their enemies, while others, burdened with the belief that they were unpardonable sinners, brought their own lives to an end by preparing and drinking a potion made from it.

The aconite also occurs in Greek and Nordic mythology. According to Greek legend, the aconite bloomed freely in the garden of Hecate, the Queen of Hades, mistress of shadows and nocturnal ghosts. In that garden the terrible three-headed dog, Cerberus, the guardian of the underworld, had picked up some of the flower's seeds on his tongues. When Hercules dragged him out of Hades towards Earth, deadly foam flew from the animal's mouths and the seeds germinated even in the most barren regions.

For the Norwegians the flower – with its distinctive little dome shape – represented in mythology the helmet of Odin, the greatest of the Germanic gods. This headgear, worn only by the lord of the warriors and by poets, was believed to endow the wearer with the magic power of becoming invisible to people and then suddenly appearing among them astride a great eight-legged steed with two wolves and two deer at his side.

Many names were subsequently given to the aconite in Nordic countries, all referring to the flower's appearance: Thor's hat, iron helmet, battle helmet and troll's helmet. With the spread of Christianity, however, the helmet was to become the monk's hood and the flower's most widely used popular name now is the "common monkshood."

In France, the aconite is generally known as *char de Vénus* (Venus's chariot) because the shape of the flower, without the upper part, suggests a chariot drawn by doves.

The leaves and rhizomatous roots contain several alkaloids, the most poisonous of which is aconitine; this is hardly used at all as a medicine today because of its high toxicity.

Aconite

Amaranth

The feathery amaranth, with its deep colour, is one of the loveliest of all red flowers. When summer comes, its long, elegant plumes retain their beauty for many days without showing any signs of fading.

The ancient Greeks and Romans believed the amaranthus plant to be sacred. Virgil suggested to those poets who were concerned about the envy and slander of their fellow poets that they should encircle their heads with a crown of these flowers: "*Baccare frontem cingite, ne vati noceat mala lingua futuro.*" (Bind the brow with amaranth flowers, the evil tongue will cease to wound.)

The Greeks regarded it mainly as the plant of friendship. Philostratus recommended that others follow the example of those who decorated the graves of their most beloved companions with amaranth. In Greek, *amárantos* means "which does not fade," in other words something that is steadfast, unchanging, like true feelings and mutual respect. Garlands of trailing plants in honour of many of the Greek deities would be interspersed with red splashes of amaranth, in the hope that the gods would not only deal indulgently with the people but would protect them too. It was to ensure her own protection that Diana, goddess of the woods, a fearless rider and skilful huntress, had the nymph Helichrysa adorn her with some of the lovely plumes that retained their colour for so long. (The flower popularly known as "immortelle" or "everlasting flower" derived its botanical name *Helichrysum* from this mythological young woman.)

Between the seventeenth and nineteenth centuries it was thought that the plumes, when crushed and sewn into small fabric bags, would bestow physical well-being and prolonged youthfulness when pinned on clothes. The amaranth thus became the symbol of immutability – of love that has no end. Perhaps this association with endless love led to this amaranth's common name of "love-lies-bleeding." More likely, though, the designation refers to the drooping plumelike flower spikes. Another common name is "tassel flower."

Amaranth

Poppy Anemone

Often referred to as "windflower," implying that it only opens when touched by a breeze, the anemone probably owes its name to the Greek word *ánemos* (wind).

Its brief period of blooming was regarded as significant by both the ancient Greeks and the Victorians who associated anemones with waiting and, thus, hope, but also with disappointment and desertion. Towards the end of the nineteenth century, it became the fashion in England to connect the word "anemone" with *"anima"* – a Latin word referring to the breath of life – and thus with the sufferings of those of more heightened sensitivity. This probably gave rise to the flower's association with low vitality and emotional, rather than physical, illness. However, medicinal properties, which will help to cure a number of ailments ranging from fever and bruises to emotional problems of love, have also been attributed to the anemone.

In mythology, the anemone is connected with Chloris, the goddess of flowers. Having discovered that her husband, Zephyrus, was passionately in love with the nymph Anemone, and had been unfaithful to her, Chloris dismissed the girl from her retinue. To spite his wife, Zephyrus asked Aphrodite, goddess of love, sex and fertility, to turn the nymph into a flower, so that his jealous wife would always have to tend her lovely rival.

Another Greek myth has anemone flowers springing from the blood of Adonis. In the Holy Land, where the anemones are red and heavily perfumed, Christian legends tell of the flowers having been bespattered with drops of blood as they fell at the foot of the Cross. The poppy anemone, which is native to the Mediterranean region, was a very fashionable flower through the final decades of the nineteenth century right up to the 1920s. It is still a fairly popular florist's cut flower. Other wild species of the anemone flower in early spring along woodland edges in the cooler regions of North America, Europe and Asia. In southern Europe, there is a sky-blue anemone with numerous petals, rather like a daisy.

Poppy Anemone

Snapdragon

The ancient Greeks called this familiar flower by two names: *antírrhinon,* from *ánthos,* flower or shoot, and *rhinós,* nose or nostrils, and *kynoképhalon,* dog's head; the German name is *Loewenmaul* (lion's throat) and in French it is *muflier* (from *muffle,* the face or muzzle of an animal). In English, of course, it has become a "snapping" dragon.

All these names refer to two attributes of the plant: the first to the way in which the flower opens like a mouth when pressed on each side; the second to the shape of the seed-containing capsule, which has two symmetrical holes rather like the nose of an animal.

In medieval times a young girl would wear a snapdragon in her hair to show that she meant to refuse the advances of an admirer. This tradition has undoubtedly given rise to the meaning that is often attributed to it today, implying "I couldn't care less." Someone wanting to show total indifference to a person might therefore present him or her with a bunch of snapdragons.

Snapdragon

Aquilegia

There are several versions of the origin of this plant's name. One is that it derives from the Latin *aquila* (eagle), as the flower's spurs resemble an eagle's claw. Another version is that the name stems from the Latin word *aquilegium,* a water vessel, perhaps because of the drops of dew and rain that are held by the leaves.

The common name for the aquilegia, however, is columbine, which clearly relates to the Latin *columba,* dove, traditional symbol of peace. Indeed, some kinds of aquilegia, when viewed from above, give the impression of doves grouped in a circle, with their tail feathers pointing upwards. This attractive image is reflected in the following poem, *To a Columbine,* written in the early twentieth century by Hywel Caerlieon:

Gentle Lady Columbine,
What a witching grace is thine!
Slender branches hung anon
With a flowery carillon;
Fretted leaves beneath thee spread,
Hornèd cap upon thy head,
Purple, rose, or golden shine
For thy vesture, Columbine.

Erstwhile there enfoldeth thee
Vestal robes of purity,
White doves brooding in the sun
(Thus the ancient legends run);
There as in a quiet nest,
Happy thoughts may fitly rest,
Peace hath made thy heart her shrine,
Fairest Lady Columbine.

It is difficult to find any references regarding its third name, *herba leonis* (lion plant). However, a legend says that in handling the flower one may suddenly acquire the strength of a lion.

Because of its rather bizarre appearance, this flower has come to symbolize extravagance, especially in Anglo-Saxon countries. In the language of flowers the aquilegia speaks of capriciousness – even flirtatiousness – eccentricity and also of passionate feelings.

Aquilegia

Arbutus or Strawberry tree

It was Pliny the Elder, the great Roman naturalist, who gave this flowering and fruiting tree the botanical name of *Arbutus unedo* that it still bears today. The arbutus is also known as the strawberry tree after the red strawberry-like fruits that often develop while the tree is also flowering.

Arbutus means "shrub" and *unedo* is a contraction of *unum* and *edo* which means "I'll eat *one* of them," implying "but no more" – clearly an allusion to the edibility, but rather unpalatable taste of the fruit. In Algerian markets the arbutus is sold in small bottle-shaped baskets, probably because in Algeria, as in Corsica, a light wine is made from the fruit. In the recipe for arbutus wine it is recommended that the crushed berries be allowed to ferment, at a temperature of 12-14°C (54-58°F), after which an equal quantity of boiling water should be added. This can then be distilled to make a kind of aquavitae. According to Jean-Louis-Auguste Loiseleur-Deslongchamps (1774-1849), the French botanist, more than a thousand barrels of it were distilled on the coast of Dalmatia in 1817.

Blackbirds, thrushes, blackcaps, magpies, robins and pigeons eat arbutus berries and thus tend to aid distribution by unwittingly sowing the seeds in migration. It is more than likely that the self-sown plants that have sprung up in the British Isles have arrived in this way although the tree is considered truly native in parts of Ireland. The Romans attributed magical qualities to the arbutus. In the *Aeneid* Virgil says that the branches of arbutus were placed on graves as a propitiatory offering to the supernatural powers.
The meaning to be read into a gift of arbutus branches is that the donor holds the recipient in high esteem.

Arbutus or Strawberry tree

Asphodel

Several plants share the common name of asphodel and even a similar appearance, but they belong to different genera. The asphodel (*Asphodelus cerasiferus*), illustrated on the opposite page, is also called silver rod, an appropriate name because of its white flowers borne at the top of tall, sturdy stems. Another asphodel, similar in looks and growing habit but having yellow rather than white flowers, is widely believed to be the asphodel of Greek mythology. Other common names for it are king's spear, Jacob's rod and asphodeline (botanically it is *Asphodeline lutens*). Both of these asphodel species are native to southern Europe, but are sometimes seen in gardens in more temperate regions. Still another legendary asphodel – the flower of early French and English poets – is believed to be the daffodil or narcissus.

The ancient Greeks regarded the asphodel as symbolizing the dead's immortal souls. Homer, in a beautiful translation by the eighteenth-century poet, Alexander Pope, dreamed of a serene afterlife amidst the lush green of a meadow covered with asphodels:

To rest at last where souls immortal dwell
In fields that ever bloom with asphodel.

According to Theophrastus, the Greek philosopher who succeeded Aristotle as president of the Lyceum in Athens in the third century B.C., the asphodel plant's roots, stems and seeds were edible. This may explain the Greek custom of planting asphodels on the graves of the dead so they could feed on the roots.

The ancient Greeks gave their earthly sufferings mythological interpretations, attributing their woes not only to the gods in order to be able to accept them with more resignation, but also to the more modest dead, perhaps as an effort to derive a better understanding of such woes. The Greeks believed that their shadows wandered through the Elysian Fields, those never-ending meadows carpeted with asphodels, and drank from the Lethe, the river whose waters induced forgetfulness of the past.

The asphodel flower was especially associated with the goddess Persephone, and her husband, Pluto, who was also known as Hades. The couple were the caretakers of the underworld, receiving the dead at the start of their journey. Persephone was also associated with agriculture and its recurring vital cycle of plant growth from seeds. Pluto obtained Persephone, his future queen of the underworld, by godly trickery. The story goes that one day, as Persephone strolled through the plain of Enna in Sicily, she stooped to admire a flower, rather like a narcissus, that was growing in her path. As she stretched out her hand to pick it, a great gaping hole suddenly opened in the ground and Pluto emerged from it. He clasped her in his arms and carried her off in a golden chariot to the nether regions of Avernus, where she became his wife and queen. In the language of flowers, the asphodel is believed to be the bearer of regrets, even beyond death.

Asphodel

Aster

Asters are the glory of the late summer and autumn gardens when their tall, imposing modern hybrids, often known as Michaelmas daisies, come into bloom. They are usually grown in borders in combination with chrysanthemums and are especially popular in the British Isles, Canada and the USA. Their colour range is varied and, in addition to white, includes rose, pink, red, purple, and lavender-blue varieties. Another common name for the aster is starwort. Carolus Linnaeus (Carl von Linné), the indefatigable eighteenth-century Swedish naturalist, named the genus after the Greek word *aster,* which means star, because of the shape of the flower's corolla.

Although the late summer and fall Michaelmas asters (mostly hybrids of the North American *Aster novae-angliae,* the New England aster, and *A. novi-belgii,* the New York aster) are exceptionally showy, as the examples on the facing page indicate, lower-growing, seemingly delicate species are native worldwide. One of these smaller wildings is the Italian starwort (*Aster amellus*), which was mentioned by Virgil in his fourth book of *The Georgics* because:

Often are the altars of the gods adorned
With its twined garlands ... and shepherds gather it in the valleys
Cropped by their flocks near Mellas's winding stream.

It was undoubtedly this Italian river that inspired Linnaeus who chose the specific name of this species, *A. amellus*.

There are several hybrids of this Italian starwort, a well known one in English and American gardens being "Mauve Cushion."

The China-aster (*Callistephus chinensis*) is sometimes confused with the true aster, but it belongs to a different genus and is an annual that must be renewed in the garden each year from seeds. It is native to China.

The aster signifies unpredictability.

Aster

Daisy

The daisy is believed to have certain prophetic qualities. Young girls in love, even today will pluck each petal off a flower, repeating "he loves me, he loves me not," as she does so. This delightful game probably developed around two particular species which belong to different genera. These are the little wild daisy (*Bellis perennis*) that grows in short grass and the much taller white dog daisy (*Chrysanthemum leucanthemum*) that grows in longer grass. The latter is also known as the oxeye or field daisy, and is a close relative of the chrysanthemum. Both types have numerous petals, which make the game last a tantalizingly long time.

The small pink and white daisy is often known as the English daisy although it is found in many countries, and is probably the first flower that most children in the world get to know. There is an old English saying to the effect that when one can put one's foot on seven daisies, summer has really arrived.

In the Middle Ages, ladies would demonstrate publicly that they were loved and that they returned that love by allowing their knight to decorate his shield with two daisies.

The same flower may, however, have sometimes conveyed quite a different message. If a lady was not sure of her loved one's feelings or had not made up her own mind whether to accept his advances, she would wear daisies on her brow.

As a symbol of purity, freshness and simplicity, the daisy pays homage to these three pleasing virtues.

Daisy

Calendula

Although often known as the pot marigold, the calendula, which takes it name from the Greek word *kaléo* and the Latin *calendae,* both meaning the first day of the month, is not related to true marigolds. Originally from the Mediterranean region, the calendula is a popular summer garden flower in more temperate areas. Where winters are mild the calendula blooms nearly all the year round, hence the origin of its name in relation to the regular passing of time. Even its habit of opening each morning at the same time and closing with the setting sun, as it does wherever it grows, gives the impression that it is a sort of calendar.

There is a strange contradiction, however, between the reality and symbolism of this flower. It is cheerful in appearance with its closely packed, sunny coloured, slender petals. Infusions and tinctures can be made from the flowers and leaves, as well as from the powder of its dried petals, which have a beneficial effect in the treatment of various ailments. A juice is also produced which acts as a strong disinfectant on ulcerations and wounds. Soothing eye-drops are also made from the flowers. And yet, in spite of so many positive attributes, the calendula is the symbol of suffering. The ancient Greeks represented pain in the form of a young man, with suffering on his face, holding a crown of these flowers in his hand. This seems to have originated from the pain felt by Venus on the death of Adonis, the flower having sprung from her tears. Calendulas, however, do not cause trouble in themselves but, when received as a gift, their silent message tells of the sufferings of unrequited love.

Calendula

Camellia

A camellia bloom has an imperturbable quality that is due both to its compact, almost sculptural, form and petal arrangement.

It was the favourite flower of Alphonsine Duplessis, the courtesan who was immortalized by Verdi as Violetta in *La Traviata,* and by Alexandre Dumas Fils as Marguerite in his famous autobiographical novel, *La Dame aux Camélias* (1848). This beautiful flower is linked irrevocably to the tragic life of the book's main character, a doomed consumptive. It has been suggested that the camellia was chosen by Dumas as a symbol of cool detachment, an indispensable attitude for one who trades in love.

Following the success of Dumas' book, the popular appeal of the flower increased. Elegant ladies would wear one on their bosom, at the waist or just above the hem of their dress, while the more dedicated Don Juans sported a blossom in the buttonhole of their tail-coats.

The first camellias were not imported into Europe until the mid eighteenth century. Brought over from China, Japan, Formosa, Korea and Burma, where they were found to be growing wild, camellias were for many years regarded as purely a greenhouse shrub, as it was rightly believed that they would not be able to survive the cold winters of central and northern Europe.

After having been in fashion for about a century, tastes changed and interest in camellias waned. A few collectors continued to cultivate them, however, including a Milanese doctor, Luigi Sacco, who created 120 new varieties between 1790 and 1820. But by about 1910 a number of keen gardeners had begun to grow them again and, by the 1930s, camellias had become an indispensable part of gardens throughout Europe, the British Isles, and the Southeast and Pacific Coast of the USA.

It is not widely known that the small, brown, aroma-laden leaves of tea that we take so much for granted come from a species of camellia (*Camellia sinensis*). It may well have been the subtly reviving qualities that an infusion of these leaves gives, that led to the flower being given a particularly subtle symbolism, the quality of modesty, or in other words, that superiority does not need to be displayed. A rare virtue indeed, it is possessed by too few people. The gift of a camellia flower is an expression of esteem and admiration.

Camellia

Bignonia or Trumpet vine

Several shrubby vines are known as trumpet creeper or trumpet vine or bignonia and at one time, most were grouped under the same generic name, *Bignonia*, before being separated into different genera. Joseph Pitton de Tournefort, a seventeenth-century French botanist created the name bignonia as a tribute to one of his contemporaries, Abbé Bignon, who was librarian and preacher at the court of Louis XIV.

Among these various trumpet vines, which are rather similar in appearance and do belong to the same family, the *Bignoniaceae*, are the very hardy trumpet creeper, *Campsis radicans*, and its named hybrid "Madame Galen." Another is the cross-vine, *Bignonia capreolata*, a native of the southern United States and not quite as hardy as the trumpet creeper. A transverse slice of this vine's woody stem reveals the marking of a cross, which gives it its common name. Yet a third bignonia is the trumpet bush or yellowbells, *Tecoma*, a genus of about four or so species more shrubby than vinelike. The trumpet bush is native from Florida to Mexico and South America and not hardy in the North.

In Mexico as well as in South America, the tropical bignonias can be seen growing by the doorways of homes, as they are regarded as sacred and propitiative to good luck. The bright red, orange or yellow flowers are used to decorate churches during religious ceremonies.

The wish expressed in giving bignonia flowers is connected with surprise and conveys the hope that the recipient of the flowers will be blessed by an unexpected, unhoped-for fortune.

Bignonia or Trumpet vine

Cornflower

This is a very ancient flower and there is evidence of its existence dating from the Neolithic period. The flowers in shades of blue are often to be seen contrasting with red poppies in cornfields in nineteenth-century paintings. Other common names for the cornflower are ragged sailor, bachelor's-button, and ragged robin. There are a number of legends that have grown around this flower, whose scientific name is *Centaurea cyanus*. According to the oldest, Flora, on finding her beloved Cyanus dead in a field full of cornflowers, wished that the flowers be named after her lover. The generic name *Centaurea* actually originates from Cheiron, the centaur, who healed a wound on his foot, after it had been injured by a poisoned arrow shot by Hercules, by applying juice made from pressed cornflowers.

According to a popular Russian and Byzantine legend, a handsome young man who had been drawn into the arms of a nymph, was changed by her into a cornflower. In the East, when a young man gives a cornflower to the object of his affection, it is to express his hope that she will accept his advances.

Described in some countries, especially in the nineteenth century, as being a plant of spells, the cornflower denotes great happiness in the language of flowers.

Cornflower

Wallflower

In its natural environment the wallflower tends to grow in groups, covering well-weathered old walls and rocks. Its fairly woody stems support spikes of colourful flowers ranging through various shades of yellow, gold, flame, chestnut brown and violet. In the sixteenth century it was grown mainly for its perfume and nearly a thousand years earlier it had been the favourite flower of the Emperor Charlemagne.

The wallflower is often grown near beehives where it attracts swarms of bees.

The wallflower has long been popular in Britain in the gardens of country cottages. Rock gardens and walls offer sites that are almost the same as its natural habitat. The plants are also used in perennial borders and as bedding subjects where their splendid displays of richly coloured blooms also fill the spring air with a delightful fragrance.

A romantic Scottish legend tells the sad tale of two young lovers who lived in the thirteenth century. Elizabeth, having refused to marry the man chosen for her by her father, the laird, had been imprisoned in the highest tower of the castle. She was in love with another young man, one Scott of Tushielaw, and had decided to elope with him. The fortunate suitor, disguised as a strolling minstrel, had composed a serenade which he sang under the windows of the prison, contriving in the words to make clear to his loved one the day and time of their flight. Elizabeth, to show that she understood, threw a wallflower down to him. When the time came to escape, however, the hapless girl slipped, sliding down over the wall which was covered with a profusion of the yellow flowers, and fell to her death. Scott remained inconsolable for the rest of his life; he composed ballads about his lost love and was never seen again without a wallflower in his hat.

In the following poem the English poet Robert Herrick tells the same story in verse, but with a different ending. To make the death of Elizabeth seem less abrupt and tragic, he made her live again in a plant with sweetly scented yellow flowers – the wallflower.

Why this flower is now call'd so,
List, sweet maids, and you shall know.
Understand, this first-ling was
Once a brisk and bonny lasse,
Kept as close as Danae was;
Who a sprightly Springall lov'd;
And to have it fully prov'd
Up she got upon a wall,
Tempting down to slide withall;
But the silken twist unty'd,
So she fell; and bruis'd, she dy'd.
Love, in pitty of the deed,
And her loving lucklesse speed,
Turn'd her to this plant we call
Now the Flower of the Wall.

This legend probably accounts for the flower acquiring the meaning of faithfulness in misfortune. More recently, however, it has tended to be associated with disdain.

Wallflower

Greater Celandine

The Latin name, *Chelidonium majus,* from which the English name derives, stems from the Greek work *chelidón* (swallow) because the plant's period of growth coincides with the arrival and departure of the swallows. There was also a very old popular belief that the swallows would rub sprays of celandine on the eyelids of their newly-hatched young to help open their eyes, hence the old-fashioned name of swallowwort. Whether it was the physical contact or some special curative property in the leaves and flowers which was supposed to improve failing eyesight or eradicate warts, is not known, but the Latin peoples certainly knew of the phenomenon and called it *Hirundinara.*

In 1570 Ulisse Aldovrandi, the Italian naturalist and ornithologist, wrote that, even in the Middle Ages, this flower had been regarded as possessing miraculous powers; he based this on his own interpretation of the derivation of the name, maintaining that far from stemming from the Greek *chelidón* it actually derived from the Latin *coeli donum*, "a gift from heaven."

These flowers are believed to be the bearers of joy and relief from worry and melancholy.

Greater Celandine

Wintersweet

Challenging the cold late winter weather, the flowers of the wintersweet (*Chimonanthus praecox*) gleam like waxy yellow stars on their stiff, sturdy stems. Their golden colour and strong, sweet perfume are welcome signs of life granted by nature in the otherwise often bleak landscape of this season.

Such a flowering occurrence must have seemed like a miracle indeed to the writer of this legend: Hungry and tired and half dead with cold, a robin was trying to find a tree or shrub with a safe branch on which to rest before continuing his flight to warmer climes. One after another, the trees showed only stubborn hostility towards him, refusing a perch to the little bird. The wintersweet, however, its branches almost bare with only a dry leaf left here and there from the fall, called quietly to him and gave him what shelter and warmth it could. God saw this kind act and, to reward the dry shrub, caused a rain of bright, sweetly scented stars to fall on its branches. This "miracle" is repeated every winter.

The giving of a single branch of wintersweet denotes tender affection, and a renewed warmth of regard; several branches tied together, on the other hand, promise warm protectiveness on the part of the giver.

If, while the flowers are still closed, some of the branches are cut and put into a vase filled with water, the buds will open within a few days. The rather stark appearance of the branches suddenly disappears under numerous reddish-brown buttons contained in crowns of yellow petals. The leaves do not unfurl until later. Wintersweet should be planted where it receives some protection as it is not reliably winter-hardy in most of the North.

The scientific name, *Chimonanthus,* derives from the Greek words *cheimón* (winter) and *ánthos* (flower).

Wintersweet

Chrysanthemum

The name of this well-known perennial plant derives from the Greek *chrysos,* gold, and *anthemon,* flower, resulting in "flower of gold," which suggests a splendid, joyous bloom. In seeming contrast, the chrysanthemum's flowers are popular and useful to the florist, particularly for funeral wreaths and other decorations because as cut flowers they are durable and resistant to wilting. This association with funerals and cemeteries has not prevented the chrysanthemum from being an important flowering plant in today's homes and public gardens, where the gold flowers, together with red, bronze, pink, lavender and white colours, make magnificent autumn displays.

Five hundred years before the birth of Christ the chrysanthemum was being widely cultivated in China and Korea, where it was greatly admired. It was introduced into Japan in A.D. 313 and the *giku,* as it was called, became the national flower of that country. Every year, when the chrysanthemums were at their best in the imperial gardens, the Emperor would hold a reception when the guests would be shown the newest varieties. Today a Chrysanthemum Festival is held each year on September 9. As cut flowers the blooms are arranged in the typical *ikebana* style in the hallway and windows of a great many houses; numerous restaurants, offices, banks, and public buildings are also decorated with cut chrysanthemum blooms and plants.

In Japan this flower has become as much associated with happiness and life as it is in China. It has been depicted throughout the ages on fabrics, porcelain and screens with drawings in Indian ink and watercolours as well as in exquisite designs in lacquer. Its beauty has been praised in poems, legends and fables.

The chrysanthemum is a comparative newcomer beyond the East. It was first brought to France in 1789 by a Marseilles merchant but it was not to arrive in England for nearly sixty years when, in 1846, Robert Fortune, a well-known plant hunter, brought home some plants with him. It had become a fashionable flower by the end of the nineteenth century and Marcel Proust describes their presence in the home of Albertine, the "girl in bloom" of his dreams.

Putting aside the superstitions with which some European cultures have burdened the chrysanthemum, the meanings that other countries have given to it are all acceptable: life, strength of mind and peace even in adversity.

Chrysanthemum

Citron

The citron (*Citrus medica*) is a small tree, which originates in Asia and was introduced to Europe by the Arabs travelling from place to place in their sailing ships and caravans. Pliny the Elder knew it well and referred to it in his botanical studies. It is often depicted in Greco-Roman frescoes and mosaics.

When Francisco Alvarez, the Portuguese chaplain, returned from travels abroad in 1513, he described a wonderful monastery garden in northern Africa where he had seen the most magnificent citron trees.

Still in the sixteenth century, the Sienese doctor and botanist, Pierandrea Mattioli, wrote of the citron: "… it is gathered by perfumers to make several kinds of scent. They carefully distill the water, which is not only more delicate than all other waters but is also very useful in medicines."

Citron peel and the entire fruit are both candied and their oil is extensively used in the making of perfumes. The citron symbolizes capricious beauty or sometimes discretion as is shown in the following lines, taken from a poem by Maria Gisborne, a friend of Shelley:

As woman's meek wisdom, their white blossoms smile,
The promise of a golden fruitage.

Citron

Orange

Because of the unparalleled beauty of this plant both when it is in
bloom and when its fruit is ready to pick, the orange tree (*Citrus
sinensis*) has always been regarded as representing good fortune.
In Chinese writings it is referred to as a good luck symbol. A number
of writers in China, its country of origin, have revealed the ancient
methods of cultivation that have been used throughout the Far East
since about the sixth century B.C.
Up to the twelfth century, a large consignment of oranges would
always leave Peking at the beginning of every year bound for the
Foochow temples to be used in sacrifices to the gods. A gift of
oranges on the first day of the year was considered a token of
happiness, prosperity and plenty.
The orange has also been used by witches and sorcerers, in
England and in Italy, to represent the hearts of their victims. One of
the most nefarious ways in which the orange was used in sorcery
was for the name of the unfortunate subject to be written on a label
and pinned on to the fruit; this was then thrown on the fire. As the
orange burned and decomposed, the victim's end was assured.
Happier associations also relate to orange blossoms, however, and
their use in decorating bridal gowns, head-dresses and in bouquets
dates back to the time of the Crusades. The Crusaders had brought
back from the Orient the custom of a bridegroom presenting orange
blossoms to his prospective bride on their wedding day. This also
reflected the Saracen tradition, according to which the flowers were
a symbol of fertility, in that they heralded such wonderful fruition.
The custom of using these white, waxy and beautifully scented
flowers for weddings continued in Europe and the United States for
a very long time. Today other types of white flower are used instead,
favourites being the white bouvardia, which is very similar to
orange blossoms but does not bear edible fruit. Stephanotis is
another popular alternative. In Crete and Sardinia – two of the most
beautiful islands in the Mediterranean – it is still the practice to
sprinkle a few drops extracted from crushed orange blossoms over
the heads of the bride and bridegroom.
There is a legend in Crete which tells of a girl who had nothing of
any value to wear on her wedding day. But, nothing daunted, she
entwined orange blossoms in her hair and decorated her wedding
dress with them too, to give the effect of rare jewels.

Orange

Clematis

Some kinds of clematis grow wild in hedgerows and woodlands in many regions of Europe and North America adorning the countryside with their dainty flowers and fluffy seed heads. It is not surprising therefore, that in the British Isles, these mostly vining plants are called "traveller's joy" and, when in seed, "old man's beard." North American species are called "woodbine" and "virgin's bower." Cultivated varieties have been grown in English gardens since the eighteenth century but the clematis really came into its own in the Victorian era.

In 1765 William Cowper, the English poet, wrote these lines, which were inspired both by a clematis and by the woman who was looking after him:

Thrive, gentle plant! and weave a bower for Mary and for me,
And deck with many a splendid flower thy foliage large and free.

Clematis was regarded as the bringer of good luck because of its light-hearted appearance and prolific flowering habit. In the nineteenth century, country people would cut the longest sprays and place them around the edges of a field in the hope of getting a good harvest. At one time, gypsies would rub the stinging juice produced by some of the wild varieties on their skin to invoke the pity of passers-by and be given alms.

There is no trace at all of any legends or associations that might account for the symbolism of the clematis, which is mentioned in a number of books: one is lucid, honest intelligence and the other, which is completely the opposite, artificiality. The name of clematis comes from the Greek *klema*, a vine branch.

Clematis

Lily of the valley

There is a medieval Christian legend that links the lily of the valley with St. Leonard, the favourite saint of Clovis, King of France. The saint, with great compassion, looked after prisoners, interceding with the king on their behalf for their release. Although his efforts were often successful, Leonard found life at court too alien and soon chose to retreat into the country to preach. He built a wooden hut for himself and every day gave thanks to God for His wonderful gifts of trees, plants and animals.

At times, the devil would appear to Leonard in the guise of a dragon, ready to fight him in order to regain supremacy over the territory that he maintained as his particular dominion. The Evil One stared hard into the saint's eyes, and long flames shot out of his mouth in an attempt to provoke him. Leonard, absorbed in his prayers, took no heed.

During one of these assaults, the flames had burned the hut and the kneeling saint risked being covered in ashes. Not until he had finished his prayers, however, did Leonard turn to face the dragon to show that he was ready to fight. And the contest raged fiercely. It continued for three days and both combatants were wounded several times, many drops of blood falling to the ground from the devil and the saint alike. But, while those of the dragon turned into poisonous plants, each drop of Leonard's blood became a lily of the valley.

Before long, the whole forest was covered with these little white, sweet-smelling flowers just as the conflict was coming to an end with the triumph of good over evil. The treacherous dragon, choking on a wooden cross that had become stuck in his throat, was burning in his own flames.

The lily of the valley (*Convallaria majalis*) is the flower that blooms in spring to announce the end of all worry and the return of serenity. It is said, too, that the nightingale waits for the first lily of the valley to bloom in the spring before flying into the woods to begin his courting.

Lily of the valley

Crocus

This little flower is one of the first to come into bloom in our gardens at the end of the winter. Various kinds of crocus also grow wild in the mountains of Europe and have always been widespread throughout the Mediterranean region as far as the Balkans, Asia Minor and North Africa. In these natural habitats, it is an uplifting experience to see the snow gradually melting in the pasturelands being replaced by a carpet of white yellow and purple flowers. The Greeks knew the crocus well and it was, in fact, the Greek philosopher and botanist, Theophrastus, author among other works, of *The History of Plants,* who gave the flower its name. It is derived from the Greek word *króke,* meaning "filament," because of the long stigmas that emerge from the center of the flower. Homer, in his detailed description of the bridal chamber of Jupiter and Juno, tells of the many types of flower that were strewn over the floor. One of these was the crocus, which, at that time, was associated with passion and sexual love. There is also a legend, possibly dating from as far as the ninth century B.C., which relates how Hermes, the Greek protector of travellers and wayfarers, fell in love with a young man called Crocus and turned him into the flower we now know by his name.

The Romans placed the crocus on graves because it symbolized hope in the next world. It is likely that our ancestors were especially familiar with the crocus (*C. sativus*) from which saffron is obtained. From it they made an ointment, which was then made into love philters. Because of this association, the crocus was also known as the "flower of the night" and bridal beds were often covered with its strongly aromatic stamens.

Saffron, still much used in the kitchen today, is a very costly commodity; it takes about thirty thousand flowers to obtain half a kilogram (approximately 1 pound)! The references in ancient literature to the association with passionate love had, by the latter part of the nineteenth century, been superseded by a new association. In the eyes of the Victorians the crocus had become the symbol of carefree youth and it is this meaning that is still given to this little flower today.

Crocus

Cyclamen

In the third century B.C., Theophrastus wrote in his *History of Plants* that the cyclamen excited love and sensuality. Two meanings have been attributed to the name of this flower which derives from the Greek word *kúklos*, a circle. There are those who maintain that, because the plant was believed to have the power to facilitate conception, the name "cyclamen" was chosen because the shape of the flower is reminiscent of the female uterus. Others see a reference in the name to the spiralling of the flower stem, which bears the seed-filled capsule, down to the soil level. Originally from Cyprus, Rhodes, Crete, the Middle East and North Africa, *Cyclamen persicum* is the large-flowered species commonly grown as a pot plant. The common name of the wild species is "sow-bread" because pigs are known to eat the enormous roots greedily, quite unaffected by the poison they contain. In the past, cyclamen plants were thought to have healing properties against a stronger poison than their own, namely snake-bite. This gave rise to the belief that a flower with such powerful properties must be magical, that it could ward off witches' spells and even influence the course of affairs of the heart.

It is not known just how the plant was used. Essence of cyclamen is believed, by some, to bring good luck. In the language of flowers the cyclamen is the symbol of diffidence. This rather surprising attribute, in contrast to all the positive references, is believed to derive from the poison contained in the roots.

Cyclamen

Dahlia

The transfer to Europe of dahlias from the botanical garden of
Mexico City in 1789 was both complex and difficult. Even their
name was hard for Europeans to pronounce, for it was the old Aztec
name of *cocoxochitl*. It is not even known which were the first
dahlias to bloom – the plants that the director of the botanical
garden in Madrid had succeeded in obtaining or those grown from
the seeds sent to German botanists in Berlin.
A great many tubers rotted or shrivelled, both in transit and during
the first attempts at cultivation in Europe. The first dahlia tubers
reached England in 1789.
The current name of this plant is derived from that of Dr Anders
Dahl, a Swedish botanist and disciple of Linnaeus, who provided
Europe with its first dahlia seeds. Not long after, in Berlin, dahlias
were called *georginen* after the St. Petersburg botanist, Georgi.
Goethe had a passion for these flowers.
In France, the Empress Josephine was filled with the same
enthusiasm and was the only person in Paris to possess some
plants. She grew them in the gardens of Malmaison, which caused a
great deal of envy. One of the court ladies, who was pregnant,
wanted very much to have one of the tubers, perhaps in the belief
that it would be good to eat. She pestered the Empress continually
to grant her this favour but to no avail.
This constant refusal eventually spurred the lady to help herself to a
few of the tubers with the cooperation of her lover and the gardener.
They were discovered and expelled from court. The Empress then
lost her enthusiasm for dahlias and no longer wanted to own and
care for them.
It is evident from the number of known recipes that sought to make
them appetizing that the tubers were once tried as food. However, it
seems they have a very poor flavour.
If, in the future, it becomes possible to transform the insulin
contained in dahlias into glucose, instead of fields of sugar-beet we
might cultivate this splendid flower on a vast scale.
Several dahlia species were used to produce the varying flower
forms and sizes in their dazzling colours that have evolved into the
modern dahlia. One species, *Dahlia pinnata,* formerly classified as
D. variabilis, is an important parent of today's hybrids and may be
why the flower is associated with instability.
Other symbols connected with dahlias are gratitude and good taste.

Dahlia

Datura

Thorn apple, angels' trumpet, jimson weed, and Indian apple are among the common names given to various species of datura. *Datura stramonium* is one of the better known species and probably native to North America, but now grows wild in many parts of Europe and Asia.

It is an annual plant with a bushy habit and fairly soft stems. Its strikingly large, white flowers, shaped rather like a five-sided funnel and almost lilylike, are delightfully scented. In the warmer climate of southern Europe, tree forms of this and other species of datura flourish on sites sheltered from the wind.

When ground into powder, datura leaves are believed to cure spasms, asthma and convulsions. The datura's walnut-sized fruit, which is covered in spines – hence the popular name of "thorn apple" – contains numerous rough, black seeds.

Pulverized, these seeds have the same properties as the leaves but to a much greater extent and they are therefore highly poisonous. The *nightshade* family to which datura belongs, contains a number of similarly dangerous members as well as several very well known ones, which we use in our everyday lives. Black (or deadly) nightshade, mandrake and henbane, all rich in alkaloids, are the dangerous ones but the drugs obtained from them, if used correctly, can be beneficial; these plants are also grown solely for the beauty of their particularly abundant flowers. Familiar members of the family are tobacco, the tomato and the potato.

The psychotropic properties of drugs obtained from *Datura stramonium* and other species – to produce escape into imaginary worlds far from reality – have been known since ancient times. Datura plants are known to have been grown near the Delphic temple, enabling Greek priests to use the drug to achieve a state of trance during religious ceremonies. In the Middle Ages, gypsy bands, wending their way across Europe from Russia, would leave behind various recipes for the drug, including medicinal ones, which were often wrongly remembered or misused. In China, it became illegal to add stramonium, one of the drugs obtained from datura leaves, to alcoholic drinks, because of its excessive use – and presumably dire effects. In Central and North America, random tribes of Indians, known as "diggers," because they dug roots for food, used the drug to procure prolonged hallucinations during orgiastic religious rites. Another common name of *D. stramonium* is Jamestown weed, after the bizarre behaviour of British soldiers who had tasted the drug in the colonial Virginia settlement.

What meaning can such a plant, which has so many properties hold for us? Perhaps magic, enchantment and bewitchment?

To receive the datura as a gift means that the recipient can expect great changes, which the donor will bring about.

Datura

Carnation

Linnaeus was the Swedish botanist who, between 1730-1770, codified the system of naming plants, which is still in use today. For this well-known flower he chose to combine two Greek words, *diós*, a god, and *ánthos*, a flower, to form the generic name, *Dianthus*. (The carnation's botanical name is *Dianthus caryophyllus*.)

Greek mythology tells how Diana, goddess of hunting, met a handsome young shepherd boy, as she was wandering through the fields and woods, and immediately fell in love with him. It was not long, however, before her feelings had changed. In a fit of rage, the capricious, wayward goddess tore out the boy's eyes and flung them down at the side of the road. Shortly afterwards some splendid blooms appeared on that spot – carnations.

Throughout the centuries, these fragrant flowers have played a part in many historical events and numerous tales have been told in which they were involved. One of the best-known stories tells how the troops of the King of France, Louis IX (St. Louis) were decimated by an outbreak of plague during the Tunisian crusade of 1270. For many of the soldiers, among whom was the king himself, the agonies of their death throes were relieved by an alcoholic concoction made with carnations. This treatment was still being used three hundred years later in Elizabethan England where it was regarded as a valuable panacea for a number of ailments. Not only was it strongly aromatic but it was believed to act as an antidote to a high fever.

There is also a Christian legend, which probably stems from the story of Diana the huntress. It tells how Mary wept at the sight of the crucified Jesus, her tears falling to the ground where the drops became carnations.

In eighteenth-century France, it was said that Marie Antoinette, imprisoned during the Revolution, used to receive messages rolled up among carnation petals. One day, as some of these flowers were being delivered to her cell, a small piece of paper fell to the ground and was pounced on by a guard. It was a plan for the queen's escape, which was thus foiled, and the unfortunate woman could not avoid going to her death at the guillotine.

One of the seventeenth-century Bourbon princes, Louis II, Prince of Condé, was nicknamed "The Great Condé," because he was a distinguished military leader. His enemies were not only the Spanish but also probably the most powerful man of the time, Cardinal Mazarin. Although reputed to be an arrogant, mannerless man, he took to cultivating carnations during his imprisonment in 1650 in the castle of Vincennes.

It may well be that the stories of these two prisoners gave rise to the custom of using the carnation as symbolic of the ideology of freedom. It is used even now by some political movements as an emblem of their party. Nearly all the meanings given to carnations of various colours are connected with different aspects of love: yellow, disdainful love; pink, reciprocated love; bright red, impetuous love.

Carnation

Carnivorous plants

Commonly known as "fly-catcher plants," these carnivorous plants flourish in damp areas and bogs in many parts of the world. As the acid growing medium does not provide enough nutrients for their survival, they are adapted to finding nitrogen-rich substances in the insects they trap. Almost every feature of these plants – their shapes, structure, reddish-green colours, long funnel-like leaves with gaping-mouthed pitchers and pointed lids or slightly swollen mobile discs, surrounded by tiny fringes and a glossy viscous fluid – clearly demonstrates their trapping function.

In Europe, the sundew (*Drosera* species) grows wild in the raised boglands of the Alps and Apennines and in North America it is often found together with the pitcher plant (*Sarracenia* species) in sphagnum moss bogs. The Venus' flytrap (*Dionaea muscipula*) is found wild in bogs of North and South Carolina. The Australian pitcher plant (*Cephalotus follicularis*) exists in the Albany Swamps and King River regions, and still other pitcher plants (*Napenthes*) are native to China, Borneo, New Guinea and the Philippine Islands. Sundew plants, which are very low growing, often carpet a sphagnum bog and sparkle when the sun catches the sticky dew-like drops secreted in the glands on the leaves. The generic name *Drosera* comes from the Greek *drosos*, dew. It is the dew-like fluid that attracts and holds the plant's prey, which is digested almost entirely by means of an enzyme.

The Venus' flytrap was found in considerable numbers by an English botanist John Ellis, who moved to North America in 1760. Ellis was fascinated by the species and wrote a monograph about it in which he described it, for the first time, as being carnivorous. Other insectivorous plants, seemingly almost animal-like in shape, attract their victims not only by their appearance and colour but mainly by their extremely sweet nectar. The little creatures, imprisoned by a close array of points that line the inside of the funnels, drown in the treacherous fluid.

There are various organisms and insects including a mosquito species, however, which have a good relationship with these strange plants. These creatures spend their larval period sheltered in a plant's pitcher, where they repay the plant for their lodging by scavenging all the leftovers of insects that it has not been able to digest. This nourishment gives them enough energy to exist until it is time for their maiden flight.

These plants were once thought to possess magical powers and were believed to bring about the successful breeding of farm animals. Today, however, a more obvious meaning is attributed to them – he who lets himself be caught is lost.

Carnivorous plants

Freesia

Although the freesia, a native of southern Africa, is devoid of any history dating back to ancient times, it has enjoyed respectable popularity as a florist's cut flower in Europe, the British Isles and North America for the past hundred years or so. The forebears of today's large, symmetrical hybrids were illustrated in a botanical register as early as 1816.

The generic and common name perpetuates a well-known German botanist, Dr. F. H. T. Freese of Kiel, who decided to take up the study of freesias after a long career as a medical practitioner.

It is probably the sweet-smelling species, *Freesia refracta*, that has escaped cultivation on the French and Italian Rivieras, where it continues to grow wild in little groups under olive trees and country hedges. The large-flowered hybrids, in clear colours, are grown in vast greenhouses in Holland, Denmark and Sweden and flown to cut-flower markets all over the world. Unfortunately, breeding improvements in the size and number of flowers on each stem have reduced the fragrance carried by some colours. Usually yellow-flowered freesias are most sweetly scented and only a few stems are needed to fill a room with their delicious fragrance. Anyone whose senses have been stirred by the exquisite perfume wafted from freesia flowers will forever be under their spell.

Freesia

Fuchsia

In 1690 a French missionary priest, Charles Plumier, assigned to the district of Santo Domingo in Mexico, took up the study of plants in that country. His most sensational discovery, news of which he sent back to France with a clear and interesting description and a rather approximate drawing, was a plant which generally grows like a small tree in Mexico. Plumier named the plant "fuchsia" in honour of the celebrated Bavarian botanist, Leonard Fuchs (1501-66).
All trace of the plant was lost for nearly a hundred years but, towards the end of the eighteenth century, some specimens of it were taken to the Royal Botanic Gardens at Kew by a Captain Firth who had recently returned from a voyage to South America.
The flower was to achieve popular fame a few years later and all credit for this is said to be due to the efforts of the grower, James Lee. One day, as Lee was driving in a horse-drawn carriage through one of the smaller suburbs of London, he caught sight of a fine specimen of fuchsia in full bloom, on the window-sill of a house. He stopped the carriage, rushed to the front door and rang the bell. When the lady of the house opened the door, he asked her who had given the plant to her and, at the same time, offered to buy it at a greatly inflated price. The lady refused to part with it, saying that her seaman son had given it to her on his return from a long voyage. Lee had to be content, therefore, with a few cuttings taken from the branch ends of this unique specimen. He raised nine new plants from these in one of his greenhouses and then began to propagate them in earnest. Soon a constant pilgrimage to Lee's nursery gardens marked not only the foundation of a fortune for the grower but also the start of a new fashion in potted plants.
Because of the delicacy of its flowers with overlapping layered petals and elegant colours and the plant's overall appearance, the fuchsia is the symbol of gracefulness.

Fuchsia

Snowdrop

The snowdrop is sometimes known as the morning star of spring flowers because it is the first to bloom in the New Year – often right through the snow in northern regions. Another common name for this bold little bulb is "fair maids of February." Its generic name, *Galanthus*, is from the Greek *gala* for milk and *anthos*, flower, as the flowers of the common snowdrop (*G. nivalis*) and the few other species of the genus are pure white except for a touch of green. All are native to Europe and Asia and, once introduced to gardens, multiply and reappear year after year to brighten the winter and early spring seasons.

An unknown writer wrote this poem about the snowdrop:

You are each year's first delight, proud in the dewy glade
standing dress'd in your green of spring and virgin white.
Agleam in the light of winter moon your colours enhearten the freezing day.
So to us you foretell how all around will gleam again just as bright, just as green.

The snowdrop is linked in the Christian calendar to Candlemas, 2 February, the day of the purification of the Virgin Mary, when candles are blessed in church.

There is also a legend with a Christian origin which tells of an incident in the life of Adam and Eve. Banished from the Garden of Eden, the unfortunate pair were forced out into the world in the midst of an extremely severe winter. Battling through the howling winds, surrounded by complete darkness, every step away from their lost Paradise became more and more difficult. At last, Eve sank exhausted to the ground; she was utterly disheartened, and unable to believe that her life, from that moment, would ever be other than cold and sad like the winter.

As Eve lay on the ground unable to walk another step, an angel appeared before her. This apparition tried to encourage her by telling her that other seasons, much better than winter, such as spring and summer, would soon arrive. But Eve was so discouraged that all persuasion was in vain. Finally the angel tried another way of giving her courage; catching a few snowflakes in his hand he blew into them, commanding them to turn into flower buds as they fell from the sky. As soon as they landed, they turned into little white spring flowers. Reassured by the sight of the snowdrops, Eve's strength returned and she was able to stand up again to continue her journey.

As a sign of life, of renewed vigour after the long, grey winter, this little flower means hope.

Snowdrop

Gentian

Gentius, the last King of Illyria, reigned from 180-167 B.C. His rule was brought to an end by the Romans because he had allied himself with Perseus in the war against them. He seems to have been the first person to have discovered the medicinal properties of gentian roots and it was therefore named after him.

In the sixteenth century *Gentiana lutea* (great yellow gentian), which grows to a height of 40 inches (1 m) or more, was widely used as a remedy against the plague. Today, it is mainly used to make bitter digestive drinks and aperitifs. As a medicine it can reduce fevers and expel intestinal worms.

The natural habitat of the lovely dark blue gentian, known as the stemless or trumpet gentian (*Gentiana acaulis*) is in the mountainous areas of central and southern Europe, mainly in the Alps but also in the Apennines. The meaning that has been given to this blue gentian is "determination" – a particularly appropriate association in view of the nature of this little flower which grows only a few inches high in the mountains creeping among the stones. The nights here are intensely cold and the sun burns by day, the winds blow mercilessly and water runs off the surface of the ground as there is no soil to retain moisture. Life under such conditions is a constant battle for plant life. Another meaning has also become attached to this blue gentian, perhaps suggested by its stiffly erect bearing, which seems to challenge all opponents with: "I shall be the strongest."

Gentian

Ivy

It is the habit of ivy (*Hedera*) to cling by rootlets along the stems to the nearest upright object. This clinging habit has given rise to the ivy's association with love and friendship. Indeed, the Arabic word *heische* means love and derives from *iscloqua,* meaning ivy. According to Plutarch, the Greek biographer who lived from A.D. 45-125, anyone who touched ivy became pervaded by a kind of prophetic inspiration and a positive drive. By contrast the grape vine, which transmits feelings of exaltation, should be kept well away from those who wish to remain self controlled and clear headed. Because of some similarity of their leaves, the two plants are often depicted together in mythological scenes. Bacchus was crowned with ivy, and his thyrsus – the staff that he always carried with him – was surmounted by grape vine leaves entwined with ivy. The thyrsus, with its association with lightning and thunderbolts, was the all-conquering weapon of the gods and thus the image of Bacchus crowned with ivy can be interpreted as both symbolic of victory and prophecy.

In Germany, when young heifers are let out to graze for the first time, it is the custom to decorate their heads with strands of ivy. In Scotland, ivy was used to protect cows and their milk from the evil eye. This ubiquitous plant grows nearly everywhere in Europe and is a symbol of faithfulness. Hence, perhaps, the French saying, *"Je meurs où je m'attache,"* which, loosely translated, means "I am faithful unto death." Love and constancy, with no evil intent whatsoever in the very exclusive feelings expressed, are the meanings attributed to ivy. The following verse by an anonymous poet illustrates this:

Yes, woman's love's a holy light,
And when 'tis kindled, ne'er can die;
It lives, though treachery and slight
To quench its constancy may try;
Like ivy, where to cling 'tis seen,
It wears an everlasting green.

This plant is featured in a number of nineteenth-century songs and ballads to express faithfulness, the best known being "Just like the ivy, I'll cling to you." Ivy leaves are also used as the emblem of several political organizations, including the Italian Republican Party.

Ivy

Sunflower

The cheerful sunflower, in the structure and colouring of its huge
flowers, is not unlike an earthly sun. Its generic name *Helianthus* is
derived from the Greek *helios*, the sun. In Peru, the sunflower was
honoured as the symbol of the great Sun God. In the valley of the
Mississippi in North America, remains of this flower have been
found that are thought to date back three thousand years before
Christ.
This New World native was introduced to Europe from Mexico and
Peru in the sixteenth century in the first sailing ships to cross the
Atlantic.
Sunflowers have inspired many poets. William Blake wrote:

Ah, Sun-flower! Weary of me,
Who countest the steps of the Sun;
Seeking after that sweet golden clime,
Where the traveller's journey is done.

The Italian poet, politician and soldier, Gabriele D'Annunzio
(1863-1938), referring to the flower when the petals and seeds have
fallen, still large and dramatic on its sturdy base stem, wrote:
"...long sulphur-coloured stems, without leaves, the great discs
uncrowned with petals nor heavy with seed were borne, seeming in
their nudity like emblems of the liturgy, pale ostensories of gold."
The North American Indians used to adorn the heads of their virgins
with a sunflower; they believed it to be a holy plant, perhaps
because they were already familiar with the many uses to which its
various parts could be put.
It is reputed that Louis XIV, the Sun King, saw to it that sunflowers
bloomed every year in his garden as a tribute to his nickname.
Towards the end of the the nineteenth century, Oscar Wilde
founded the Aesthetic Movement in London which took the
sunflower as its emblem. At that time the flower was seen
everywhere – in fabric design, carved in wood, forged in metal and
incorporated into all the decorative arts.
In the language of flowers, the sunflower symbolizes cheerfulness
and pride.

Sunflower

Hellebore or Christmas rose

The hellebore is perhaps better known as the Christmas rose because of a Christian legend, which tells how, at the end of December, a seemingly delicate pinkish-white flower sprang out of the bare, frozen ground in time to celebrate the birth of Jesus. Its presence in the winter scene, with its gleaming petals and evergreen foliage, certainly earned it such a lovely name.
The name hellebore is derived from the Greek *helein,* to kill, and *bora,* food.
There are several strange events associated with this plant, one of which concerns its beneficial purgative effects. These are said to have been discovered by a Greek shepherd named Melampus as he was guarding his sheep. Realizing his discovery to be important, he told the followers of Hippocrates about it; they soon began to treat him as their equal – a scientist, doctor and healer.
An episode in Greek mythology confirms the fame acquired by Melampus. Proteus, an old sea god who lived on the island of Pharos, was gifted with intuitive, prophetic and highly developed powers of mimicry. He could take on the semblance of any animal in order to escape from his persecutors and enemies. His daughters, who had become quite confused by their father's transformations over the years, believed themselves to be cows. Only Melampus, who had been asked by Proteus to cure the young girls of their delusion, was able to bring them back to sanity and Proteus, to express his gratitude, had given Melampus permission to marry one of them.
Another legend tells how Solon, one of the Seven Sages of Greece and an eminent legislator, had suggested using the hellebore to win a battle that seemed likely to go on for too long. The city of Cyrrhus was under siege by the soldiers of its rival city, Delphi. It was decided, therefore, to throw a mass of hellebore flowers and roots into the waters of the moat that surrounded the walls and await the result. Many of the besieging soldiers drank the water, only to be overcome by such violent stomach cramps and diarrhea that, despite their determination to continue with the siege, they were forced to abandon the operation.
Recent research has shown that the hellebore is an exceptionally good antidote to mental disorders, which indicates that the legend of Proteus's daughters being cured may well have a factual basis.
The meaning attributed to the Christmas rose is relief from anxiety.

Hellebore or *Christmas rose*

Hibiscus

The Greek origins of the name of this flower derive from the word *ibískos*. Dioscorides, one of the most famous Greek doctors who lived in the first century A.D. and who had a profound knowledge of the curative properties of plants, used this name to describe the mallow, which grows wild in most of the regions surrounding the Mediterranean. It, along with the hibiscus, belongs to the *Malvaceae* family.

The tropical hibiscus (*Hibiscus rosa-sinensis*) was apparently introduced to Europe by one Ghislain de Busbeck, the Imperial Flemish Ambassador at the court of Sultan Suleiman the Magnificent in Constantinople somewhere between 1520 and 1566. During his term of office, de Busbeck developed a passionate interest in botany. In just his first year of residence in Asia Minor he sent back to Europe specimens of Persian lilac, philadelphus or mock orange, hyacinth and, of course, hibiscus.

In the Polynesian islands, and in Tahiti especially, it has always been the custom for young girls to wear a hibiscus bloom in their hair when they go dancing. Even the young men wear one behind an ear – if behind the right ear it means they are engaged to be married, but when behind the left ear, it means they are as yet uncommitted.

The hibiscus is perhaps the best known of the bird-pollinated flowers. It is particularly attractive to humming-birds which, as they hover over each flower to drink its nectar, brush against the long anthers with their wings and feathers, thus unknowingly transferring the pollen on to the stigmas. These exquisite little creatures have no need to land on the petals, leaves or branchlets, which might be too delicate to support even such a light weight. It is the silky delicacy of these blooms combined with the brevity of their flowering period that has given the hibiscus flower its meaning: a gift of hibiscus flowers is a tribute to the recipient's elegant beauty but, at the same time, a reminder of its transience.

Hibiscus

Hyacinth

The name of this bulbous, very fragrant flower probably derives from a Greco-Albanian root, *giak*, which means dark red, and the suffix *inthos*.

However, Greek mythology links this flower to a young boy named Hyacinthus who was loved for his beauty by Zephyrus and Apollo. Legend has it that, while the boy was playing in the sunshine at throwing a bronze discus, Zephyrus, the west wind god, was overcome by a fit of jealousy and deflected the flight of the discus, which caught Hyacinthus on the temple and killed him. Apollo, the sun god, not being able to revive the boy, transformed him into a flower coloured as red as his blood.

The hyacinth was beloved of the ancient poets and is often mentioned in the works of Pliny, Virgil and Theocritus. In Imperial Rome, children would wear red hyacinth flowers interwoven into little crowns in honour of Ceres, goddess of the fields. The Greek goddess of love, Aphrodite – or Venus, as she was known to the Romans – succeeded in making Paris choose her as the winner of the golden apple inscribed "for the fairest" by presenting herself to him lying on a bed of hyacinths. In exchange, the victorious goddess used all her powers to make Helen fall in love with the warrior, Paris.

The first hyacinth bulbs were brought into England in 1560 from Persia by Anthony Jenkinson and, at about the same time, they were beginning to arrive in Italy where, a hundred years later, Cosimo de' Medici ordered a large quantity for his own gardens. The Low Countries – Holland in particular – had been cultivating them for some time, ever since an Italian ship had foundered off the coast; hyacinth bulbs were scattered all over the beach and, as the sand settled over them, they grew in apparently almost ideal conditions. Problems of cultivation appeared to have been unpredictably solved.

In 1734, one single hyacinth bulb was sold at a public auction in England for the incredible figure of 134 pounds.

Meanings are attributed to hyacinth flowers according to their colour: red is the symbol of pain or sorrow; blue symbolizes constancy, and white is the symbol of discretion. All hyacinths are associated with games, sport and recreation.

Hyacinth

English Holly

The custom of decorating our houses with holly, during the Christmas season, is very ancient. The Druids used holly to deter evil spirits, and Pliny the Elder, in the first century B.C., advised all who could to plant a holly tree by their front door to protect the house from the perfidy of the wicked.

In many northern countries of Europe, too, medieval man believed that this plant was more powerful than any attacker, or storms that might blow in the long, dark winter nights.

English holly grows mainly in woods where the beech predominates, the two being ideally suited as companions as they both thrive in a similar environment.

Maté is the name of a South American holly species which originated in Paraguay, Argentina and Brazil. Slightly prickly if at all, the leaves of this species, when dried and roasted, make a stimulating infusion. It is often drunk in Peru and Brazil by sucking it through special filtering straws from hollowed pumpkins.

The English or European holly (*Ilex aquifolium*), with its sharp prickly leaves, is a symbol of strength, immortality and aggressiveness. This is probably due to its stiff, proud appearance and leathery leaves while the invigorating qualities of the infusion – which were also known to dwellers in the Black Forest in central Europe – may also have contributed to the symbolism.

English Holly

Iris

In the fifteenth century B.C., long before the Greeks had begun to take an interest in certain herbs and roots, Pharaoh Thutmose I returned to Egypt from the Syrian wars with something very unusual among the impressive amount of booty. This was a fine collection of plant bulbs, tubers, dried flowers and seeds which it was thought would be useful in various ways. A few of the species were cultivated and propagated to beautify the gardens and, once they had been analyzed by some learned doctors and healers, were found to be beneficial in the treatment of various ailments and in the preparation of love philters. In the Temple of Ammon in Thebes there is a carving dedicated to Thutmose I, who had followed the research on his plant booty with great interest, which depicts several flowers, one of which is a kind of bearded iris.

One of the deities in Greek mythology was named Iris. She was the messenger between the gods on Mount Olympus and mortals; she was also the goddess of the rainbow, her journeys being so frequent that the many coloured bridge in the sky – the contact with the beloved gods – became indispensable to mankind. The flower thus takes its name from the Greek for rainbow because its many different colours were reminiscent of this phenomenon.

The flower depicted in the coat-of-arms for the Italian city of Florence has been described as a lily but it is, in fact, the *florentina iris,* a variety of *iris germanica,* which grows quite freely in the surrounding Tuscan countryside. It is a strange coincidence that the same error is repeated in the appellation of a flower of such national importance as the lily of France. This is, in fact, an iris. It is said that Louis VII, having emerged victorious from a battle that had taken place in a marshland full of yellow iris (perhaps *Iris pseudacorus*), had been inspired by a dream the night after the action to make that flower his emblem. When the iris appeared on the King's coat-of-arms, the French called it the *fleur-de-Louis;* said quickly, however, this becomes contracted to *fleur-de-lys,* meaning lily-flower. The iris, together with the peony and chrysanthemum, is one of the national flowers of Japan.

The iris symbolizes ardour and passion. Irises in general, of any colour, are the bearers of messages, good wishes, and news.

Iris

Jasmine

The fragrant jasmine (sometimes spelled jessamine) has provided eastern writers with endless inspiration for prose and poetry. A few lines by an Indian author give some idea of its fascination and of the power of its perfume:

"A sprig of jasmine in her hair, some saffron and sandalwood powder on the head of a beloved and beautiful woman – all this is a small piece of Paradise."

Traces of jasmine found in Egypt date back to very early times. Minute amounts of its powder have been found on the mummy of a Pharaoh in the necropolis at Deir el-Bahri.

The first species to have arrived in Italy and France may have been the poet's jessamine (*Jasminum officinale*) a native of western China. Somewhere around the sixteenth century, a Tuscan noble succeeded in acquiring a specimen for his garden, but gave strict instructions to his gardener that he was not, on any account, to propagate it or to give away even one single spray. However, the gardener's fiancée disobeyed the order, took a sprig and planted it in a piece of her own ground. The cutting flourished and the girl nurtured it until she was able to take other cuttings from it; she continued to take more and more cuttings which, when well rooted and in bloom, she sold. As a result, the jasmine made her rich enough to marry the gardener and ensure their comfort for the future. It has become the custom in Tuscany for young women to add a spray of jasmine to their bridal bouquets in memory of their enterprising forebear; it is believed to bring good luck, especially to the bridegroom.

The yellow or winter-flowering jasmine (*J. nudiflorum*), which flowers between January and March, is the symbol of grace and elegance. The white poet's jessamine that blooms in the summer symbolizes amiability, although in Spain it signifies sensuality.

Jasmine

Sweet Bay

It is believed by some that the Latin name for this fine shrub, *Laurus nobilis*, stems from the Celtic word *laur*, green. Certainly its leaves are a rich, dark green and, when crushed, yield a strong aroma. The sweet bay (or bay laurel or bay tree) grows freely in all Mediterranean countries, especially between the coast and lower slopes of the mountains. Four thousand years ago in Greece, crowns of bay leaves were used to honour heroes and poets. Since then such laurel or bay crowns have continued to be the symbol of the highest praise.

Apollo himself was often represented wearing a crown of bay leaves to denote his status as a god who purifies, illuminates and triumphs. Plutarch described the distinguished Roman general, Scipio, as making his triumphal entry into Carthage bearing his scepter in one hand and a laurel branch in the other.

Magical powers have also been attributed to this plant. One belief was that it enabled the prophets to practice occultism. It was said, too, that the magic of a bay tree had given Daphne, the beautiful woodland nymph, the chance to escape from the all-too-pressing attentions of Apollo by turning into a a bay tree. Greek and Roman literature attributed very positive symbols to the laurel. Several Roman writers have described the festival that took place every year on May 15 in honour of Mercury, the god of trade. It seems that the branch of a bay tree would first be immersed in a fountain and then the water caught on its leaves was sprinkled over the merchandise to ensure that all the goods would be sold.

In times nearer our own, it was the custom in some rural areas of Italy for the countryfolk to burn a few branches of the bay tree; if it burned with a crackling flame this indicated that there would be a good harvest but if the fire was silent then it would be a poor one.

In a little Sicilian village called Troina, once a year on St. Sylvester's feast day, it is traditional for all the men to ride out on horseback into the woods where they gather branches of sweet bay and, carrying their spoils, gallop in pairs up to the church door. There they break off a leafy twig and throw it to the ground; they then make their way homewards, each with the remainder of his branch which is now regarded as having been blessed.

In Corsica, too, laurel wreaths are hung on the door of the bridal chamber on a couple's wedding day to wish them happiness and prosperity.

Sweet Bay

Madonna lily

The word "lily" derives from the Celtic *li* (white). The first lilies to be distributed throughout Europe, which had originated in Syria and Palestine, must therefore have been white.

The Greeks, who regarded the shape of the flower as being particularly beautiful, with its symmetrical form of three petals and three sepals, thought that its creation was the result of divine will. The Romans, on the other hand, believed it was begotten from Juno's milk; two drops had fallen from her breast while she was feeding Hercules, one to be transformed into the Milky Way and the other into a lily. Venus, who felt that the immaculate whiteness of the flower was too dazzling, introduced yellow stamens covered with golden pollen into its calyx.

The ancient Romans used the petals of lilies, together with rose petals, to scent their beds.

The flower chosen by King Louis VII of France (1120-80) to adorn his coat-of-arms – and which was henceforth adopted by the French monarchy – has always been referred to as a lily although it is quite plainly an iris. The error seems to have arisen through the contraction in the twelfth century of Louis's name to *Lys*, which means lily.

Florence, too, has a stylized flower in its coat-of-arms that has always been described as a lily. The emblem of the city, however, was intended to be an iris, because this was a flower that grew prolifically in the extensive marshlands that lay just outside the city walls.

Within the Christian world the Madonna lily has been considered an appropriate symbol of purity in relation to the Virgin Mary. It is also associated with St. Joseph, who is often depicted with a staff from which spring lilies in full bloom. There is a legend, clearly inspired by the chastity of their union, which tells how Mary had chosen her husband from among all the eligible men, after having seen him carry this unusual staff bearing her favourite flowers.

The satirical English poet, Tom Hood, in his poem *Flowers*, refers ironically to the symbolism of purity and elegance that is attributed to the lily:

The lily is all in white, like a saint,
And so is no mate for me.

Encumbered as it is with traditions, this flower represents many – perhaps too many – virtues: purity, dignity and nobility.

Madonna lily

Tulip tree

The Latin name for this handsome flowering tree is *Liriodendron* from the Greek *léiron,* lily, and *déndron*, tree. The descriptive Latin species name that makes up the rest of its botanical name is *tulipifera*, which obviously refers to its large, tulip-like yellow-green flowers.

This tree is native to North America where it grows wild from Massachusetts to Florida and west to Mississippi.

The indigenous North American people used to call the wood of the tulip tree "canoe wood," and canoes capable of carrying up to twenty people could be carved out of a single trunk. These Indians also made an infusion from tulip tree bark to counteract attacks of fever. The bark, when reduced to scales in water, releases a substance called liriodendrine, which has the same heat-reducing qualities as quinine.

As this plant was originally native to the United States, it is not surprising that between the eighteenth and twentieth century more than one meaning came to be associated with it – modesty, reserve or self-restraint and sensitivity. This tendency to relate the tree to rather restrained meanings probably derives from the colour of the flowers. Although they are most beautifully formed and have a delightful perfume, they remain basically pale greenish and tend to blend with the foliage, being only noticed on close inspection.

In regions where the tulip tree grows freely, blossoming branches are often used to decorate churches for weddings. Not only are the blooms lovely in themselves but they also bring with them the unspoken hope that the relationship between the bride and bridegroom will always be one of mutual respect and gentleness.

Tulip tree

Magnolia

The bull bay or southern magnolia (*Magnolia grandiflora*), a large stately evergreen tree, grows wild from North Carolina to Florida and west to Texas. This pride of America's southland has a high rating among the other distinguished trees and shrubs of this genus, which are mostly native to Asia. (Flowers of the bull bay, along with those of a Chinese species, *M. quinquepeta,* are shown on the facing page.)

It was said in Georgia, sometime in the nineteenth century, that a magnolia tree was as necessary to a fine house as the pillars that supported it.

The complexion of Scarlett O'Hara, the famous heroine of Margaret Mitchell's novel *Gone with the Wind*, set in Georgia, was likened to the white petals of this magnolia's flower.

The tree was noticed by the French botanist Plumier during his search for new plants on behalf of Louis XIV on the other side of the Atlantic. It was he who chose the name as a tribute to the scientist Pierre Magnol. Not until 1740 did the first specimen of the magnolia arrive in France, when it was taken to Nantes by a merchant trading between Europe and America.

There is a delightful story told about one of these plants which had been growing rather unsatisfactorily for a few years in a greenhouse because the gardener believed it needed to be protected. When the magnolia was eventually exposed to the fresh air by the gardener's wife, in whose care it then was, it immediately improved and continued to grow and flourish for a hundred years or more.

It is said that the gift of a magnolia means that the donor is either seeking to express his or her own sense of dignity and perseverence or to recognize these qualities in the recipient.

Magnolia

Chamomile

The delicate, daisy-like flowers of the chamomile have long been known as the ingredients of a soothing tisane, which helps to combat anxiety and insomnia. At one time, they were also regarded by gardeners as the ideal companions for other, weaker and less healthy, plants.

Clumps of chamomile would be planted in sunny positions as close as possible to ailing trees and shrubs. The more skilful growers would even eliminate the particularly strong-growing chamomile plants so that the "patients," rather than becoming too dependent on them, would build up their own resources. It seems, too, that the aroma given off by chamomile leaves is not only beneficial to nearby plants but is also pleasant and healthy for people.

Its long flowering period, which can last from early summer to autumn, makes the chamomile ideally suited to covering fields that would be difficult to maintain as meadowlands. In more formal situations it is used as a substitute for grasses to make a lawn that can be trod upon. The plants are considered essential in herb gardens. In July, when the flowers are at their best, they are dried by exposing them to the air but avoiding direct sunlight.Chamomile flowers are associated with the meaning of "strength in adversity," probably because of the calmness that the tea or infusion, already referred to, is able to generate.

It is well known that distinctive types of pollen have given many botanical research workers and archaeologists just the clues they have needed to complete certain types of work. In Iraq, for example, the skeleton of a Neanderthal man was found in a vegetal stratum which, on examination, was found to consist of mountain flowers. It was later discovered, too, that several of the species discovered in that grave had hallucinogenic properties. Traces of chamomile pollen were found in the bandages wrapped around the mummy of the Egyptian Pharaoh, Rameses II. This had probably been slipped in with the intention of imbuing the Pharaoh's spirit with the strength and calmness needed to face the long afterlife.

The various plants known as chamomile have been bounced from one genus to another, but the best known botanically is *Anthemis nobilis.*

Chamomile

Forget-me-not

This tiny flower bears a heavy responsibility indeed, for it stands for "faithfulness." There are two legends about it, which come from very different cultures, that extol the principle of faith in eternal love. They have also secured its place in everyone's heart and given rise to its common name.

The first, from Persia, tells of an angel who had fallen desperately in love with a young mortal girl and had therefore been banished from the Garden of Eden. While he was still weeping unconsolably, Allah summoned him to give him the chance to expiate his misdemeanour and return among the blessed. The only condition was that the whole world should be planted with forget-me-nots. The angel confided to his loved one that he was afraid he might not succeed in fulfilling this, but she, who was prepared to follow him on his long journey, reassured him. Allah, touched by the love of the two young ones, decided to welcome them both into the Garden of Eden.

The second story, which comes from Austria, is both romantic and tragic. As two young lovers were strolling along by the Danube, they noticed some little flowers, as blue as the sky on that sunny day, floating on the water. The young man, in trying to reach them from the bank, fell into the river and, just as he was about to be swept away by the powerful current, cried out to his grief-stricken companion, "Love me… never forget me!" This legend was very well known in Europe and festivities of all kinds were held during the forget-me-not's flowering period.

Early in the twentieth century, wealthy Europeans would arrive in Luxembourg to attend the balls where beautiful girls would dance barefoot with wreaths of sky-blue flowers in their hair. These festivities took place on the banks of two small rivers, which were rather imaginatively called, "the fairies' bath" and "the oak tree waterfall."

The generic name of forget-me-not is *Myosotis.* It is derived from the Greek *mus,* a mouse, and *otes,* an ear, which refers to the shape of the leaves.

Anyone who gives a posy of forget-me-nots is making a declaration of his or her feelings.

Forget-me-not

Myrtle

The ancient Greeks believed that those who grew or gathered myrtle (*Myrtus communis*) would have energy, vigour and power. So, too, would those who wove sprays of myrtle into crowns for their heads or to decorate their clothes and home.

In Athens it was only the writers of love poems, victorious warriors and the best athletes, who wore crowns of myrtle. A symbol of love and vitality, this shrub or small tree was believed to have special powers. It was also believed that whoever touched it would be smitten by a new, enduring passion.

The myrtle was very dear to Venus, goddess of beauty and love, and it was also the favourite plant of Myrrha, the daughter of Cinyras, King of Cyprus. All the married ladies, who attended the celebrations in honour of the plant, were offered a myrtle branch so they could make bracelets, anklets and a crown from it; these were supposed to restore desire and imagination in amorous relationships as is illustrated in the following couplet by J. H. Wiffen:

The myrtle on thy breast and brow
Would lively hope and love avow

The Greeks believed that Aphrodite, having emerged naked from the sea, covered in foam and with a group of satyrs in her wake, had found refuge in a myrtle wood. Because of this, the shrub was dedicated to her.

In England, it is still the custom to include a sprig of myrtle in a bride's bouquet to express the wish that the couple's love will be complete.

Myrtle

Narcissus

The story of Narcissus, the handsome young shepherd whose father was the river god Cephisus, is beautifully told by Ovid in Book III of his *Metamorphoses*.

The boy, Narcissus, was so fascinated by his own beauty that he did not even notice that all the young girls of the forest, nymphs and dryads alike, were in love with him. And the nymph who adored him the most was Echo. Although she received nothing but total indifference in return for her devotion, in desperation she followed Narcissus wherever he went. Days and years passed while the lovesick nymph wasted away to a skeleton in the hope of winning him.

Eventually the gods took pity on Echo and ended her torment by turning her emaciated body to stone, for by this time her mind and spirit had become detached from reality. Turned to stone in the midst of meadows that had witnessed her ceaseless attempts to attract her beloved, she now pleaded with Fate to change the hostile course of events so that Narcissus would finally notice her. It is said that her voice still sounds in the valleys, reverberating over the rocks where her unhappy life had been lived.

In the meantime, the handsome shepherd boy still enthralled by his own beauty, saw and heard nobody. One day, kneeling by a pool to drink, he bent over its motionless mirror of water and saw his own face reflected in it. So struck was he by such beauty that he remained transfixed, in rapt admiration of his own reflection.

At first, Cupid tried to make Narcissus aware of his folly. He put make-up on the youth's face and tousled flowers and leaves in his hair but to no avail. Eventually the little god of love gave up in disgust and left him alone in his ecstasy of self-contemplation.

It was only Echo who heard the sighs and groans with which Narcissus bid his agonized farewells to himself. As he frantically sought the image that had slipped away from him, he had fallen into the water where he struggled blindly until he drowned, still hoping to recover that perfect face as he had seen it. All the nymphs made a funeral pyre but Narcissus' body melted away as the flames began to lick round it; in its place was found the flower that now bears his name and which, when its bulbs are planted by a pool or stream, bends its head down to be reflected in the water.

In his book *Natural History*, written between A.D. 66-77, Pliny the Elder describes the narcissus or daffodil as a plant with narcotic, or at least soporific, qualities in its strong perfume. The etymological root of the name confirms this hypothesis, as the Greek word *nárke* means "torpor."

This flower has acquired the following meanings: self-satisfaction, conceit, egoism and an inability to love other people.

Narcissus

Lotus

Eastern peoples regard the flower of the lotus (*Nelumbo nucifera*) as a symbol of perfection, purity, the sun, the sky, creation, the past, present and future. It thus represents life itself as well as the greatest virtues that should accompany it. In the Hindu and Buddhist religions it is treated as a sacred flower. In Hindu temples the god Brahma is depicted supported by a lotus flower and Indian Buddhists visualize Buddha's seat as being shaped like a broad version of the sacred flower. Indians say that the breath of Vishnu, lord and god of the universe, is perfumed with lotus, that his navel is in the form of the flower and that, when the god wishes to move from one place to another and to rest at the same time, he is transported on nine gilded lotus flowers.

In ancient Greece it was the emblem of beauty and eloquence. In the thirteenth of thirty *Idylls,* written by Theocritus of Syracuse between 300-250 B.C., there is a description of how the girls wove lotus blossoms into Helen's hair on the day of her marriiage to Menelaus.

In Egypt, it used to be the custom to place a lotus flower on the genitalia of female mummies, probably in the hope of obtaining purification and regeneration.

This magnificent plant, known as the sacred or East Indian lotus, grows in many temperate areas around the Mediterranean, although it is native from southern Asia to Australia. There is an exception in northern Italy, however, where the climate is distinctly cool. This is on lake Superiore, near Mantua, which is covered with lotus leaves and flowers, thanks to a young natural science graduate who, in the 1920s, experimented with acclimatizing lotus rhizomes from Japan. The results of his efforts can still be admired today.

The gift of a lotus flower expresses the great admiration of the donor for the recipient.

Lotus

Oleander

In the Italian region of Tuscany, the oleander is sometimes referred to as "St. Joseph's staff." This is because local legend has it that all the young men who were vying for the hand of Mary in marriage had to place a stick on the altar; when Joseph made his offering of oleander wood, it immediately burst into flower and he won his bride. In India the oleander is a funeral flower and everyone in that country knows the heroine of Tagore's play, *Red Oleanders*, who kills herself wearing a crown made of interwoven flowering branchlets. It may be because the whole of the plant is poisonous that the oleander is often linked with cautionary proverbs. For the same reason, it used to be said in nineteenth-century Venice, *"el fior de leandro no se mete in testa perché fa cascar i cavei"* ("Do not wear oleanders in your hair or it will fall out.") Pliny the Elder wrote of an unsaleable type of honey which was regarded as poisonous because it had been produced by bees that had fed on the nectar of oleander flowers.

It had evidently still not been appreciated just how poisonous this plant was; someone may well have happened to put some of the flowers or leaves into their mouth or have tasted the juice from the wood and not have realized that it was this that had caused their subsequent serious illness or even merely a general feeling of malaise.

In Libya, the indigenous people treat abscesses with oleander leaf poultices.

It is said that the flower's scientific name, *Nerium oleander,* may derive from the Greek word *nerón,* water, and that this is a reference to the large amount of moisture the plant needs to survive, for which the roots penetrate deep into the ground.

This is not regarded as a welcome gift by anyone who is concerned about superstitions connected with flowers. The plant, however, has the great advantage of flowering profusely for a long period of time and is easy to grow in warm, temperate climates.

In the language of flowers the oleander means "diffidence."

Oleander

Waterlily

The scientific name of the waterlily, *Nymphaea*, is believed to have been derived from those virgins of Greek mythology, the nymphs, because the Greeks attributed antiaphrodisiac qualities to this beautiful flower.

There are two legends that bear witness to this theory. The mighty Herakles (or Hercules) was deeply loved by a nymph but his totally indifferent response made the poor young girl die of her infatuation. The Greek god, his feelings of guilt at last breaking through his coldness, changed the nymph into a waterlily. The second legend is similar but the parts are reversed. A nymph called Lati took on the appearance of a waterlily in order to escape from the attentions of Priapus, the deity who, to the Greeks, represented the sexual instinct.

The common theme in these two tales is unrequited love linked to a personification of purity and coldness or, better still, of platonic love.

The ancient Egyptians chose the waterlily for its beauty alone, as the most suitable flower to be painted on the walls of the Pharaohs' tombs.

In the Orient, people were particularly attracted to a trait peculiar to some varieties, of opening their flowers at sunrise and closing them at sunset. This accounted for a custom which once existed in Egypt in honour of the god Osiris, who was killed and hacked to pieces by his brother, Set, and then brought back to life by his wife, Isis, who put all the pieces of her husband's body together again. Therefore, statues of Osiris were always crowned with waterlilies because his resurrection symbolized the dawn – the arrival of the sun.

(However, some varieties of waterlily open their flowers at night.) Purity, chastity and coldness are the virtues associated with the waterlily.

Waterlily

Orchids

The orchid was called *kosmosándalon* by the ancient Greeks, meaning "sandal of the world," because of the unusual shape which often occurs in some species that grow wild in the Mediterranean area. The inflated lip really does look rather like the toe of a little shoe, which has resulted in such common names as lady's slipper and moccasin flower. The ephebes, the most handsome young men in Athens, took part in certain festivals when, dressed in white, they would sing the praises of the gods with crowns of orchids on their brows.

The strange shape of all the species in this vast family – with the asymmetrical corolla that seems anxious to expose its reproductive organs and which sometimes takes on the likeness of insects, animals or human beings – has given rise to the belief that orchids have aphrodisiac powers. The ancient Greek physician, Dioscorides, advised the childless to eat orchid tubers as a remedy for sterility.

The Roman naturalist, Pliny the Elder, formulated a theory of his own according to which orchids, with their resemblance to beetles, were a cross between insects and flowers. In much of medieval Italy the native species were believed to contain the same fecund properties as had been attributed to them centuries before. The roots, in fact, were used in the making of philters and elixirs of love.

Orchids

Orchids

When the intrepid hunters of a century or two ago undertook exploratory voyages to the Far East as well as Central and South America, they penetrated tropical forests where they faced tremendous privations in order to obtain even one single new specimen.

Gustave Wallis, for example, crossed the Andes several times, finally reaching a height of five thousand meters (16,400 ft.); he followed the course of the Amazon River until he found himself in Ecuador, by which time he had lost his mind and eventually died of a fever.

The demand for new species was so great and the prospect of financial rewards so high that men were driven to undertake dubious if not crazy ventures. In 1870, for instance, a Prussian had bought an unknown species of lady's-slipper orchid from a tea planter. It was a particularly attractive plant in shades ranging from jade green to violet. Having procured his plants, he then tried to destroy the whole of the wild colony in order to be the sole producer.

At about the same time, an orchid plant valued at thirty thousand pounds had at last been successfully brought to flower in England. Orchids were being priced at astronomical figures because it was impossible to reproduce them from seed. It was not until 1905, in fact, that Noël Bernard discovered that germination only took place when the seed came into contact with a particular type of fungus. This was because orchid seeds, unlike the seeds of nearly all other plants, were found to have no reserve of food and depended entirely on the fungus for nourishment.

Orchids

Orchids

Reaching out on a graceful stem, each flower opens wide to display
its radiance, colours and strange shapes, the different varieties
exuding their own perfume and lures to attract bees and flies,
butterflies and mosquitoes, moths and hummingbirds, even bats –
a whole army of creatures, which unwittingly brush against the
blooms and carry pollen from one flower to another.

Considered to be rare and difficult to grow, orchids have always
been a symbol of refinement and luxury. An orchid is given by one
person to another in unspoken recognition of and in homage to his
or her sensuousness and elegance.

In the first volume of his novel *À la Recherche du Temps Perdu,
(Remembrance of Things Past),* Marcel Proust describes the way in
which Odette, Swann's future wife, surrounds herself with orchids:
"She found something 'quaint' in the shape of each of her Chinese
ornaments, and also in her orchids, the cattleyas especially (these
being, with chrysanthemums, her favourite flowers), because they
had the supreme merit of not looking in the least like other flowers,
but of being made, apparently, out of scraps of silk or satin. "It looks
just as though it had been cut out of the lining of my cloak," she said
to Swann, pointing to an orchid, with a shade of respect in her voice
for so 'smart' a flower, for this distinguished, unexpected sister
whom nature had suddenly bestowed upon her, so far removed
from her in the scale of existence, and yet so delicate, so refined, so
much more worthy than many real women of admission to her
drawing room."

Orchids

Corn Poppy

Opium is widely used as a soporific drug in India and Iran. In China, before it was forbidden by the Communist regime, it was smoked by a large proportion of the population. Opium is obtained from *Papaver somniferum,* an annual species with white, pink or red flowers. From opium are produced morphine, thebaine, codeine, and papaverine. Modern medicine uses these drugs in minimal amounts, to ease anxiety and pain. The wild red poppy with its erect, hairy stem, that we associate with corn fields, is *P. rhoeas* (illustrated on the opposite page), which has always grown here and there in many parts of Europe and Asia. Among its common names are field poppy, corn poppy and Flanders poppy.

The nineteenth-century English art critic and writer, John Ruskin, was fascinated by the red flowers of the corn poppy that grew among the ruins in Rome. He described the flower as intensely simple and floral, all silk and fire. At the end of the First World War, the poppy became the traditional flower of remembrance in the British Isles of those who gave their lives for their country.

Two episodes in Greek mythology which were also taken up by the Romans, involve the poppy. Demeter, the divinity who watched over the fields of grain, found comfort in her grief for the abduction of her daughter Persephone by Hades, the god of the underworld, through drinking infusions of poppy flowers. The ancient Greeks used to offer crowns of poppies to Morpheus, the god of dreams and one of the thousand sons of Hypnos, the god of sleep, to demonstrate their devotion to him; he was regarded as the great consoler of human woes. (In both myths the poppy was probably the opium species rather than the corn poppy.)

In the ancient Egyptian tombs of 1,000 B.C. it was customary to place garlands of poppies by the mummies of young princesses to wish them a happy eternal sleep.

The different colours of various poppy species have given rise to some imaginative interpretations; the pink poppy is associated with serenity and happy dreams, the red with soothed pride and the variegated with surprises and premonitory dreams.

There are several meanings for the poppy in the language of flowers but that which recurs most frequently is "consolation."

Passion Flower

Geranium or Pelargonium

François Masson, a follower of one of the most dedicated of plant hunters, Joseph Banks, is believed to have been the first European to have shipped pelargoniums or geraniums, as they are more popularly known, from South Africa – fifty kinds in all – towards the end of the eighteenth century. According to other authorities, however, the pelargonium is supposed to have arrived in Amsterdam in 1609.

The tender pelargoniums and the hardy geraniums of perennial borders and rock gardens have some features in common and do both belong to the *Geraniaceae* family, but each has its own genus – *Pelargonium* and *Geranium*. It has become common practice to refer to them all as geraniums, although many people prefer to call the common geranium, pelargonium. Their seeds are easily confused, as both resemble the beaks of wading birds; this is reflected in their nomenclature as the word pelargonium derives from the Greek *pelargós,* a stork, and geranium from *geránion,* which means the beak of a crane. True geraniums are hardy plants with striped petals while the tender pelargoniums can be distinguished by the two upper petals of each flower being slightly larger than the others.

After the great success pelargoniums enjoyed in the nineteenth century, especially in Victorian England, the idiosyncracies of fashion caused them almost to disappear from private gardens and they were described as being fit only for decorating the streets. However, the qualities of pelargoniums are so outstanding that today they are one of the most popular of all flowering plants. They are appreciated for their long flowering period, their resistance to dry summer weather and their particular suitability in urban and suburban areas for balconies, window-boxes, patio containers, and as bedding plants.

Not all pelargoniums are admired solely for their bright flowers. Some kinds have delightfully scented foliage – the peppermint geranium *(Pelargonium tomentosum)* and lemon geranium *(P. crispum)* being two well known examples. The leaves of the sweet-scented rose geranium *(P. graveolens)* are added to finger bowls and used to make jelly and to flavour summer punches.

There is a legend about the origin of the geranium or pelargonium which relates to the prophet Mohammed. It is said that, at the end of a tiring day of preaching and prayer, the founder of Islam had washed his djellabah and spread it out to dry in the sun over a mallow plant, one of the commonest in the Middle East. When Mohammed removed the dry garment a few hours later, he discovered that the plant that had been covered by the cloak had changed into a magnificent pelargonium.

Geraniums have several meanings, depending on their colour and shape: the ivy-leaved geranium denotes an inclination for a permanent relationship. The dark red geranium represents melancholy. The pink geranium means particular attention and preference.

The oak-leaved geranium expresses warm feelings of friendship. The red geranium brings thoughts of comfort and consolation.

Geranium or Pelargonium

Petunia

The petunia originated in Brazil, and its name was chosen by the
French botantist Antoine-Laurent de Jussieu in 1803. No one knows
what this plant was called by the indigenous people but they used
the word *petun* to describe the nicotiana or tobacco plant, which is
somewhat similar to the petunia and in the same family.

A botanical explorer, Philibert de Commerson, who had braved the
dangers and discomforts of South America, first noticed this prolific
flowering, rather sprawling plant. Large, ferocious cats such as
jaguars must have been a constant threat to exploring botanists
while flies, wasps, ticks, lice, ants and bats – especially of the
vampire type – dogged every expedition. After climbing the most
inaccessible mountains and reaching the edge of dense forests, an
area which required great courage to penetrate, this brave man
discovered the petunia.

Today's often sweetly scented, brightly coloured petunias dominate
seed catalogues and are a familiar sight in our gardens and
window-boxes. The petunia is a boon to gardeners for it produces a
prolific succession of flowers for several weeks and will repeat the
show if straggly stems are cut back in midsummer.

Petunias are the symbol of love that cannot be hidden.

Petunia

Potentilla

The Latin name *Potentilla* is formed from an etymological root, *potentia* meaning power, and the suffix *illa,* a diminutive which gives the whole word the implication that there is a lot of force or power in a small plant.

Members of the genus are commonly called cinquefoil or five-finger and include mostly hardy species that are native to Asia, Europe and the Americas. Some are charming little plants that hug the ground, but there are also low shrub types.

The potentilla acquired its name because of its medicinal qualities. An infusion of the leaves of one of its species, *P. anserina,* the silverweed, was used as a tonic while the rhizomes of *P. erecta syn. tormentilla* were, at one time, used in powdered form to make a strong astringent medicine for cholera. *Potentilla reptans,* cinquefoil, is still in use today as an astringent decoction in cases of upset stomachs and as a gargle. In the past, it was used to combat fevers and soothe ulcers, sores and wounds.

The symbolic meaning of potentilla is maternal love. It may be derived from the characteristic of one of the species to close its leaves over the flowers to protect them from the rain, just as a mother would defend her children from unexpected calamities. An anonymous Victorian poet wrote this delightful little poem:

How gracefully the Potentilla throws
Its trailing branches down the rude bank-side,
Until they kiss the wavelet as it flows
O'er pebbles polished by the crystal tide;
Nor there alone it grows, but far and wide
Its quinate leaves and golden blossoms lay,
And deck the borders of each rural way.

Potentilla

English Primrose

For twenty-one years, starting in 1860, every spring day saw a bunch of primroses arrive at Benjamin Disraeli's front door. This remarkable British statesman and novelist, who was born of Jewish parents of Italian origin had once mentioned in Queen Victoria's presence that his favourite flowers were primroses. From the next day, until his death in 1881, the sovereign made sure that he received a regular bouquet whenever they were in season. Her last gesture to her friend and loyal supporter was to arrange for some of the famous primrose plants from Osborne House, the royal residence on the Isle of Wight, to be planted by the palace gardener on Disraeli's grave.

As a token of respect to their late leader, Conservative members of Parliament have continued to wear a primrose in their buttonhole on April 19, the anniversary of his death, and the Primrose League was founded in England to commemorate his work and continue to promote his political principles.

The prolific number of blooms with which this early-flowering and apparently delicate little plant *(Primula vulgaris)* confronts adverse weather conditions, has been an inspiration to many people. It represents the essence of spring and is seen as an example of those hopes of renewal, which this most vital season of the year brings with it. The following verse taken from Sydney Dobell's poem, *A Chanted Calendar,* shows this hardiness:

First came the primrose,
On the bank high,
Like a maiden looking forth
From the window of a tower
When the battle rolls below
So looked she,
And saw the storms go by.

Its medical qualities may also have contributed to the high esteem in which the primrose is held. Its dried petals and rhizomes can be made into infusions to relieve migraine and into decoctions to help clear irritations of the respiratory passage. Rather than using primroses as a medicine, Disraeli served young tender shoots of the plants as a salad. They were first soaked in salt water, then drained and boiled for ten minutes or so. As a salad, they were served with a vinaigrette sauce and decorated with a few of the yellow flower heads.

English Primrose

Flowering Cherry

In the first century B.C., Licinius Lucullus won a victory over Mithridates at Pontus on the shores of the Black Sea. During his stay, Lucullus tasted cherries for the first time and developed a passion for them. The city of Kerasus offered him some plants to take back to Rome and the species thus became known as *Prunus cerasus,* the sour or pie cherry.

Frescoes and mosaics depicting cherry leaves and fruit have been discovered in southern Italy in both Herculaneum and Pompeii. Pliny the Elder was able to identify at least nine kinds of cherry. The Germans and Danes maintained that demons hid in cherry trees surrounding the fields to ward off anyone who might approach with the intention of stealing. In Finland, centuries ago, the red colour of cherries was the symbol of a bride's lost virginity. In England it was said that a dream of cherries was a warning of a forthcoming misfortune.

The learned doctors of the famous Salerno school of medicine in southern Italy suggested, at the end of the Middle Ages, that, "…the cherry purges the full stomach, and its stones cast out gallstones and make good blood flow in the veins again…"

There are many references in literature to the cherry. The English poet A.E. Housman wrote:

Loveliest of trees, the cherry now
is hung with bloom along the bough,
And stands about the woodland ride
Wearing white for Eastertide.

The Japanese express their admiration of cherry blossom in some of their loveliest, very short *haiku:*

The Cherry blossoms fall
on the still water of the rice-field:
stars in the dim light of a moonless night.

But look!
words are needless
before the cherry trees in bloom
on Mount Yoshino.

The lower slopes of Mount Yoshino in the Nara region of Japan, a short distance from Tokyo, are covered with about a hundred thousand wild cherry trees. When these are in bloom, it is a sight which the Japanese will travel many kilometers to see.

In Chinese legends, the cherry is identified with female beauty and sexuality. In Japan, apart from gracefulness and charm, it is the symbol of integrity, courtesy and modesty: a great many qualities for a small tree. More recently, a cherry blossom has come to have a meaning of its own, initiated in the Victorian era and continued to a certain extent up to the present day. This has no particular connection with Western tradition but stems, perhaps, from what was gleaned in the nineteenth century about the Japanese formality of gesture and life generally. It has become the symbol of good manners and politeness, qualities to be admired and imitated.

Flowering Cherry

Flowering Peach

This small tree originated in China, and arrived in Europe via Persia. In 331 B.C., Alexander the Great, in conquering Armenia, had the peach tree carried as far as Greece. Some examples eventually arrived in Italy. There is a fresco in Pompeii in which some white fruit, thought to be peaches, are depicted.

A number of parochial account books have been found in England, dating from the time of the compilation of the Domesday Book (1085-86), in which some unusual payments were entered for the tending of peach trees, well known to be among the most delicate of fruit trees.

The sixteenth-century Italian pharmacologist and botanist, Pierandrea Mattioli, described peaches as being "of yellow colour and very scented," various methods of cultivation being already in operation at this time. Another sixteenth-century figure was the naturalist, Castor Durante, who, in his *Herbario novo* (New Herbarium), recommended an infusion of peach blossom and the juice of peach leaves as a remedy for worms. He also made some suggestions for producing plants with better blossom and bigger fruit: "To make peaches grow larger, the smallest and weakest fruits should be removed, so that the remaining ones, having more nourishment, may become bigger."

Beethoven, a few days before he died in 1827, wrote a letter to an Italian friend, asking him to send him some peach jam, of which he was particularly fond.

In Egypt, the peach leaf has been chosen as a symbol of silence because of its long, pointed shape, rather like a tongue.

The peach has special meaning in both the East and the West. In China, it represents immortality and the spring; the Chinese god of longevity is portrayed making his first appearance by emerging from a peach.

To give peaches is an expression of admiration for the qualities and fascination of the recipient. To receive peach blossoms means that the recipient can rely on the total devotion of the sender.

Flowering Peach

Pomegranate

Solomon sang of an "orchard of pomegranates," in the Old Testament. Linnaeus, the great Swedish naturalist and botanist, chose the name *Punica granatum* to describe the small, thorny tree that is the pomegranate, perhaps because he believed that the plant originated in North Africa, *Punicus* or *Peoniceus* meaning Phoenician or Carthaginian. It may also have been chosen because he knew how the Romans had praised the ripe fruit they had found in Carthage, saying it was the most delicious in the whole of the Mediterranean area. The pomegranate probably originated in southern Asia but it has long been naturalized in southern Europe. There is a legend that explains the origin of the pomegranate – it is also one of the oldest tales on the subject of incest. It is said that a widower had fallen in love with his young daughter and that she, to escape from him, had chosen rather to die. The gods changed her into a tree – a pomegranate – that would produce more flowers and glorious fruit than most others. At the same time, the gods turned her father into a sparrow-hawk, making it quite impossible for any of this species of bird ever to perch on the thorny branches of a pomegranate tree.

In Turkey, it is the custom for a young bride to throw a pomegranate on to the ground; the number of seeds that emerge as the fruit splits is supposed to be the number of children she will bear. In Dalmatia, when a suitor asks for the hand of the girl he wants to marry, he must transfer a pomegranate tree from his future in-laws' garden to his own.

In the language of flowers it is said that the lovely red pomegranate flower represents passionate love. Both the fruit and the flowers are the bearers of heartfelt messages. Because of the large number of seeds contained in each fruit, it has always been regarded as a symbol of fertility and therefore of wealth.

Pomegranate

Alpenrose Rhododendron

The name rhododendron, after the Greek *rhodon,* for rose, and *dendron,* tree, was used by Pliny, but it was for a different shrub, the oleander. As late as 1576 the error was continued, with the oleander again being called rhododendron, in a French book. True rhododendrons, however, were known then, especially the alpenrose (or alpine rose) *(Rhododendron ferrugineum)* of the Alps (shown on the facing page), but it was not until 1629 that true rhododendrons, long disguised under lengthy, confused descriptions produced by herbalists, were suggested as shrubs for garden use.

Much of the confusion over this beautiful shrub finally ended in 1753 when Linnaeus classified the genus as *Rhododendron,* including the nine species then known. (Today, over 800 species are known, their places of origin scattered over the world except for Africa and South America.)

Fossilized remains discovered in China, the Caucasus and in North America bear witness to the fact that the rhododendron is a very ancient plant. Rhododendrons were known to have been in cultivation in oriental gardens in the seventeenth century.

In the mid nineteenth century, forty-three new rhododendron species arrived from the Himalayas with an expedition, which had set out from England under the guidance of the botanist Sir Joseph Dalton Hooker (1817-1911).

A little later, another botanist, George Forrest (1873-1932), was sent out to the Far East by the Royal Horticultural Society where he and his party were involved in an incident in Tibet, which nearly cost them their lives. They had entered by force what was then the "forbidden" holy city of Lhasa and a group of fanatical Buddhist monks had followed them with the obvious intention of killing them, once they were off sacred ground. They were spared, however, and Forrest remained for many years in the Chinese province of Yunnan from where, out of a total collection of about four thousand plant species, the expedition finally brought home to England a large number of rhododendrons.

With such a wealth of varying species introduced by Forrest and many others, it was inevitable that highly skilled horticulturists would begin to specialize in rhododendron hybridization, which continues to this day in the British Isles, North America and elsewhere.

Because of the fragility of some species and varieties of rhododendron flowers, which can be damaged by high winds, late spring frosts and heavy rains, the rhododendron is sometimes said to symbolize the fragile moment of enchantment; it is especially linked to the first declaration of love.

Alpenrose Rhododendron

Roses

Whether it has five or sixty petals, standing stiffly to attention or climbing to a great height, scented or scentless, tiny or large, half-closed or over-blown, a rose is welcomed everywhere and by everyone. The praises of the rose have been sung for over three thousand years. Learning about the rose's history and discovering how and to what extent it has left its mark on the cultures of the whole world can be most rewarding. The English archaeologist, Sir Charles Leonard Woolley (1880-1960), claims to have recognized a rose carved into stone with the early cuneiform characters, at Ur, the ancient Sumerian city-state in Mesopotamia in Asia Minor. This first reproduction of what is such a familiar flower to us now, therefore, dates the known existence of the rose from 2250 B.C. We probably owe the first coloured depiction of a rose to the refined taste and extraordinary artistic foresight of the early Greeks. This first example can be seen in a fresco in the old palace of Knossos, the ancient capital of Crete, where it is shown with other flowers around the celebrated blue bird. Many botanists have tried to identify the species of this rose with its blueish leaves but no definite conclusion has yet been reached. Possibilities include the *Rosa gallica* or *R. canina,* all of which probably grew wild in Crete. Other experts have seen many similarities to the *Rosa richardii,* which originated in Ethiopia and Egypt.

Whichever species these roses were, in order to have some in bloom for several months of the year, the Greeks speeded their flowering time by keeping them watered with warm water.

However, Lucius Junius Columella tells us that in 60 B.C. it was the practice in Rome to make roses repeat their flowering periods by pruning them before March.

The rose seems to have played a prominent part in Roman life. *Mea rosa* was the name given to a woman who accompanied returning soldiers back from the battlefront. For the priviledged few, rose-water would often flow from some of the city's drinking fountains; rose petals were floated in the wine just before it was drunk and, at banquets, showers of rose petals often floated from the ceiling onto the guests.

The pleasures and vices alike of the Roman Empire must, therefore, often have been permeated by the beauty and sweet perfume of roses.

Roses

Roses

For the Greeks and Romans and right up to the present day, the Latin phrase *sub rosa* has always meant a conspiracy of silence or tacit complicity. This originated in 479 B.C. when Greek generals held a secret conference in an overgrown rose garden to plan what was to be their victorious counter-attack against Xerxes, the Persian king. After the successful outcome of their plans, it was discovered where the meeting had taken place and roses came to be regarded as symbolizing reserve – the keeping of one's own counsel.

Midas, King of Phyrgia in Asia Minor, exiled to Macedonia in 420 B.C., obtained permission to take his collection of rose bushes with him. According to the botanist who recorded this fact, the most sensational variety was one that was quite unknown to him – it had sixty petals and was heavily scented.

Two classical poets were the first to write about roses. Sappho, in the sixth century B.C., wrote poetry on the island of Lesbos and became the first poet to celebrate the rose in verse. Then came Theocritus of Syracuse, founder of the Greek school of pastoral poetry in the fourth century before Christ, who extolled the beauty of rose gardens.

The custom, which still continues today, of planting rose bushes on graves or in commemoration of those who have been cremated, has very old origins. The rose has always been regarded as a rather special tribute to the dead.

After the fall of the Roman Empire, we have to thank a few groups of monks for many varieties of rose which have survived. For a long time, monasteries were the only places in which they were grown and tended but then at the end of the eighth century Charlemagne ordered the cultivation of a number of plants, among which were lilies and roses. There were possibly three species of the rose at that time – *R. canina, R.gallica* and *R.alba* – all of which were highly regarded for their medicinal properties.

The first version of the allegorical poem, *The Romance of the Rose*, dates from 1236. It tells of the dream of a young man in love, who hopes to conquer the object of his passion, having seen her in the form of a rose. During the long series of events in which she is involved and in which she plays the leading part in her new guise, there is not a single disparaging reference to the rose.

Roses

Roses

Always a source of delight and a symbol of strength, beauty and simplicity, rose bushes were regarded as valuable booty by the soldiers who transferred them from one end of the world to the other. At least two new species were probably brought into Europe by returning Crusaders – *Rosa gallica officinalis* and *R. damascena*. This great passion for roses continued in Europe, and two cities – Rouen in France and Florence in Italy – became keen competitors for supplying the rose market.

Cut flowers were to be seen everywhere – as decorations in people's houses, at banquets and worn by women in their hair and on their dresses.

In 1485, peace between the two English families of York and Lancaster was finally achieved. For years they had been deeply involved in the War of Succession – the Wars of the Roses – but this came to an end with a marriage between a member from each of the warring parties, Henry VII and Elizabeth of York. After their marriage, the emblems on their coats-of-arms – the red rose of Lancaster and the small, white rose of York, which had become symbols of the opposing sides – were incorporated into a coat-of-arms for the newly formed Tudor line.

A third type of rose is associated with the history of the Wars of the Roses, the *R. damascena versicolor*, which has white petals flecked with red. Legend has it that it appeared a few days before the marriage, just prior to peace being made between the two families.

In Persia, houses and mansions had interior courtyards with porticoes and enclosed gardens devoted to roses, as well as pools and fountains into which, even nowadays, rose petals are thrown on the arrival of guests. From April to May, when the oily essences, distilled waters and scented powders derived from roses are on sale in the markets, the air is heavy with the aroma of roses. The Far East has always been an inexhaustible source of wonderful plants. Vast numbers of rose bushes have been introduced to Europe over the years from Japan, China, Korea and India, borne at first on camels, horses and even elephants, later on sailing ships and finally on steamships.

Between the seventeenth and twentieth century, the owners of greenhouses and gardens, public administrators and people responsible for nursery and botanical gardens have been engaged in constant attempts to obtain specimens of the rarest plants that can be found. One of these seekers was the first wife of the Emperor Napoleon, Josephine de Beauharnais, who, between 1786 and 1814, collected a hundred and ninety-seven varieties of rose for her world-famous rose garden in the grounds of Malmaison.

Gentle sweetness, heart-break, joy, ecstasy and humility – all these feelings can be expressed with this flower, which has always been a symbol of beauty.

Roses

African violet

Besides the two main members of the viola family, the sweet violet
and the pansy, there is the African violet which is really a "false"
viola and in no way related to them.

The natural home of this familiar indoor plant is in the humid
forests of Tanzania in East Africa facing the Indian Ocean. It grows
wild among the woods and pasturelands covering the slopes of
Kilimanjaro and especially of the Usambara Mountains, at heights
ranging between 1,000 and 2,800 meters (3,300 and 9,240 ft), it has
rosettes of thick, downy leaves spread out like those in a bridal
bouquet and small, deep violet-coloured flowers with bright yellow
anthers.

The first African violets to be discovered were found by a German
nobleman, who was the district governer of Usambara and a hunter
of plants and animals. So attracted was he to the beauty of those
flowery rosettes that he carefully collected seeds and sent them
home to his father, Baron Walter von Saint Paul-Illaire, in Germany.
The director of the Royal Botanical Gardens, Herman Wendland, at
the Herrenhauser in Hanover, succeeded in growing a great many
plants from the seeds and named the plants *Saintpaulia* in honour
of the two barons, who had discovered and imported them.

African violets were first shown to the public in the 1893 Floral
Exhibition in Ghent, Belgium. Horticulturalists and nurserymen
were quick to see their possibilities as pot plants and a number of
splendid new varieties were soon produced from *S. ionantha*.
Numerous hybrids followed from crossing some of the botanical
species discovered later. Today, the African violet is the most
popular house plant in the USA and over much of the world. In the
beautiful African regions where they originated, these little plants
are associated with the idea of faithfulness and especially with the
promise that a loved one will return – a meaning which seems to
introduce a note of optimism to an expression of love.

African violet

Rowan or
Mountain Ash

This small, round-headed tree has been the subject of folk tales throughout most of Europe and western Asia for countless years. Its generic name is *Sorbus* and its specific name *aucuparia* comes from the Latin *aucupium,* bird-catching, and derives from the use to which this tree has been put since man's history began. Because birds are such gluttons for its red berries, bird hunters have habitually positioned themselves near the branches where it is easy to catch them. Men have created what might be described as bird snares by planting small woods or thickets for no other purpose than to lure their little prey into them.

In the first few centuries after the birth of Christ, the Druids – Gaulish, British and Irish priests – grew a circle of these trees around their huge votive stones to protect themselves against the spirits of the night.

In country areas, too, the rowan tree has long been the focal point of innumerable superstitions. During the Maytime celebrations in northern Europe, for example, the tree was associated with fairies and witches who were believed to be particularly active at that time of the year. Rowan branches were hung over the doors of houses and stables, as well as around the pens for cows and sheep, to give protection against devils and witchcraft.

It was also believed that receptacles full of butter or milk, when encircled with the branches of such a propitious tree, would be safe from thieves. For the same reason, rowan trees were planted along the boundaries of fields, and whips and walking-sticks made from rowan wood were believed to give protection to men and beasts alike against unforeseen dangers.

This is a tree that is believed to bring good luck. Connoisseurs of good food maintain that birds which have fed on rowan berries are particularly tasty, and experts in the culinary arts often add a few of the berries when making a sauce for game.

Rowan or Mountain Ash

Broom

Oh, the broom, the yellow broom,
lauded by ancient poets,
how sweet it is on Summer days
to lie and rest beneath your fronds.

These simple lines are by an unknown poet who knew how much
the Greeks and Romans appreciated this plant, especially for its
particular attractiveness to bees which, greedy for its pollen, made
excellent honey. Pliny relates how the Greek ethologist,
Aristomachus, who lived in the third century B.C., made a special
study of the life of bees. He grew broom to attract them and, in so
doing, created an apiary that remained very active for a good
fifty-eight years.

In Spain the yellow broom was regarded as an essential plant in
gardens, not only for its perfume but also because its root fibres
could be used to make marine ropes. In France the plant was used
to feed sheep and the stripped wood was then cut up to make
brooms, a common practice throughout the whole of the
Mediterranean.

Broom was to reach its peak of glory in the twelfth century. King
Henry II of England, a descendant of the French house of Anjou,
took the name of Plantagenet from his family's badge, namely a
branch of broom (*planta genista* – the botanical name for broom
being *genista*) .

According to a Sicilian legend, the plant is somewhat despised
because the sound of its branches in the wind disturbed Jesus while
he was praying in the garden of Gethsemane, making it easier for
his persecutors to find him.

The French king, Louis IX, who was to become St. Louis, founded
the Order of the Genista. A contemporary description gives us a
clear picture of the style of dress worn by the knights who were
admitted to the Order: they wore a white damask mantle with a
violet hood, the collar formed by a chain interspersed with genista
flowers and a gold pendant engraved with a lily.

The common name of broom is used for three closely related
genera, all members of the legume family. One common broom,
Genista tinctoria, is native to Europe and western Asia and has
escaped from cultivation in many countries. It is known as dyer's
greenwood, dyer's broom and dyer's greenweed because of its
traditional use for green-to-yellow dyes. The Spanish broom
(*Spartium junceum*), a shrub native to the Mediterranean region,
has especially fragrant flowers. Other brooms, including the
Scottish broom, (*Cytisus scoparius*), are favourite garden shrubs,
all sharing similar characteristics of mostly yellow, fragrant flowers
borne on bright green, almost leafless branches.

Perhaps because of its few needs in the dry ground in which it
grows, the two meanings attributed to broom are "modesty" and
"humility."

Broom

Tulip

The name of this popular garden flower comes from the Turkish *tulipam* or *turband*, perhaps because of its turban-like shape. Bulbs used to grow wild in Persia and cultivation of them began about a thousand years ago. According to a Persian legend the first tulips were created from the drops of blood of a disappointed lover who may have taken his own life.

It has remained the symbol of a declaration of love for many centuries. This was because, growing as it did on the banks of the straits of the Bosphorus, it was used as a means of communication between hopeful lovers and the women who were confined in the harems. The young men would gather handfuls of tulips so that they could pass messages of love through the palace grills.

The tulip festival is celebrated in Istanbul in April. In the eighteenth century all the gardens in the Levant were ablaze with tulips and it was the wish of both the Grand Vizier and the Sultan that these flowers should be used to create spectacular effects in rural festivals. At one of the most famous of such festivals it is said that the plants were illuminated by small, colourfully painted lanterns on little carts drawn by tortoises. These moved slowly about the avenues of the parklands while tiny multicoloured birds chirped all night in innumerable cages hung from the trees. Because there was no perfume in the air in these delightful places, a rain of rose petals was made to descend on the guests.

The most entertaining story of all concerns the arrival of the first tulips in the West. The bulbs were brought to Vienna in 1556 by Augier Ghislain de Busbeck, the Austrian ambassador to Constantinople, and found their way into the hands of a botanist named Clusius who at first did not know how to grow them. He planted them in piles in the ground as a result of which only one or two flowered. Then someone tried to use them in the kitchen, leaving them to macerate in sugar, while someone else threw them into boiling oil – neither of which recipe was successful!

Some time later, Venetian merchants began to receive tempting offers for transporting bulbs from Turkey to France, but it was in Holland that the most enthusiasm was to be aroused. In 1593, Clusius was invited to lecture at the University of Leyden and he took a few bulbs with him. Within the next thirty years, the price of bulbs in Holland began to soar. It is said that one bulb was exchanged for a pair of fine carriage horses complete with their trappings and a carriage. In 1637, however, a law was passed which controlled the payment to be made for tulips, bringing them into line with other merchandise. This was the end for many speculators. However, tulips became a widespread obsession, leading to some amusing episodes. For example, it was said that the Duc de Bouillon, husband of Marie Mancini (the niece of Cardinal Mazarin), believed himself to be a tulip; he made his valet water him and happily went around saying that he was growing from a bulb.

According to Persian tradition, this flower is the symbol of perfect love. Throughout the whole of the Western world, however, it represents inconstancy. One could thus give an ironical interpretation to these two apparently contradictory meanings by suggesting that perfect love is inconstant.

Tulip

Periwinkle

In the summer of 1736, Jean-Jacques Rousseau would walk nearly every morning through the grounds of the Charmettes country house, near Chambéry with his beloved patroness, Madame de Warens. This great thinker and man of letters was deeply involved with nature. During one of these walks he saw a periwinkle for the first time and was so enthusiastic about this creeping evergreen with its blue flowers that he persuaded the gardeners to plant it extensively all over the grounds.

The periwinkle (*Vinca minor*) grows wild in nearly all parts of Europe and was well known to painters and poets in the earliest centuries. It has escaped from cultivation in the eastern United States where it cheerfully carpets the ground in shade.

To the ancient Celts, who had left Germany and Bohemia to discover the rest of Europe and Asia Minor, this little plant was sacred to sorcerers and those with the power of healing. In France it is still called the *violette des sorciers*.

In many places it was once customary to strew periwinkle flowers before a bride and bridegroom. There was also the custom of entwining some of the long trailing stems into a coronet for the dead as a symbol of constant remembrance, probably inspired by the strength and sturdiness of this outwardly delicate-looking plant. The gift of periwinkle means a desire to preserve a sweet memory.

Periwinkle

Violet

From the Levant to the British Isles, woods, semi-shaded hillsides and slopes, as well as damp valleys, are full of violets, the best known being the sweet violet (*Viola odorata*). A symbol of modesty and innocence, they have been a constant inspiration to poets and writers. Shakespeare often refers to them. For instance, in *Hamlet,* Laertes puts Ophelia on her guard against the ill-considered actions of those in love:

For Hamlet, and the trifling of his favour,
Hold it a fashion and a toy in blood:
A violet in the youth of primy nature,
Forward, not permanent, sweet, not lasting,
The perfume and suppliance of a minute;
No more.

After Ophelia has drowned herself in the stream, Laertes utters:

Lay her i' the earth;
And from her fair and unpolluted flesh
May violets spring!

In *The Winter's Tale* Perdita, a sweet innocent creature, is a high born girl who has chosen to live simply with the shepherds. It is she who says:

...violets dim,
But sweeter than the lids of Juno's eyes
Or Cytherea's breath...

There is a legend, which deals with Venus – the goddess of love, beauty, fertility and nature – and her reawakening each spring. The radiant goddess had married the awesome Vulcan, god of fire and metal, but was unable to accept him fully as a husband. The marriage was only consummated when Vulcan came to Venus wearing a circlet of scented violets on his brow.
There is evidence that the Greeks used to crown themselves with garlands of violets in the hope that this would prevent them from falling prey to drunkenness. This was probably because they attributed qualities such as correctness, restraint and probity to the flower. Violets were also used to give added bouquet to their wines. The violet was one of the favourite flowers in ancient Greece and a symbol of the great city of Athens.
One of the more poetic paintings by Albrecht Dürer, in the Albertina collection in Vienna, depicts a simple violet among blades of grass. The lovely old cathedral town of Parma, in northern Italy, chose this little flower for its arms. A very fine perfume is made in Italy called *Violetta di Parma*.
Violets were the basis of the Persian sherbet, a cold drink which was much enjoyed by the ancient Romans who also fried the flowers with slices of lemon and orange. Many old recipes for violet flowers are still followed today. Two are for crystallized violets and violet candy. A gift of violets implies an expression of humility on the part of the donor, especially if the recipient is in a much more powerful position.

160

Violet

Pansy

The pansy is a close relative of the sweet violet, although generally
much larger (the Johnny-jump-up is a miniature pansy), more
brightly coloured and showy. The markings on its petals have given
rise to some strange local names such as "three-faces-on-one-
head," "herb trinity," "heartsease" (although, strictly speaking, this
is only applicable to the wild viola), "kiss-me-behind-the-garden-
gate," and others. Its common English name stems either from the
Latin *pensare,* to think, or *pendere,* to hang down; the former would
probably relate to the thoughtful expression given to the "face" by
the markings and the latter to the flower's habit of hanging down
parallel with its stem.

The oldest-known legends involving pansies come from mythology.
Io, daughter of Melia and Inachus, and a virgin priestess in the
temple of Juno, was a nymph of incredible beauty. Jupiter fell in
love with her and to prevent his wife Juno from witnessing their
clandestine meetings, he took on the appearance of a cloud. The
other nymphs were jealous, however, and betrayed Io to the
powerful goddess who changed her into a young white heifer. One
day, as the unfortunate creature was standing apart from the herd in
a field, brooding on her sad fate, she suddenly noticed that
numerous little flowers had sprung up all around her, with their
corollas facing towards her. In them she imagined she could see the
face of her beloved one. It was not long before Cybele, goddess of
earthly things, arrived to give her what comfort she could. This
goddess even helped Io to escape to Egypt where Juno would have
searched for her in vain. When Io arrived in this new country, she
regained her former beauty.

Many centuries later, some confusion was to arise in France over
the two main members of the viola family – the pansy (*pensée*) and
the sweet violet (*violette*) – in connection with the Bonapartists. It is
said that Napoleon's supporters had chosen the viola as a
countersign to enable them to recognize each other; their
organization had been forced to go underground after the emperor
had been made to abdicate in 1814 and accept the tiny dominion of
the Isle of Elba. However, it had not been made clear which of the
two main types of the viola family was meant. It seems that, even
when acknowledging his supporters before sailing for Elba,
Napoleon had said he would return "with the violets," that is to say,
in the spring. As it was, he reappeared with a small band of
followers on March 1, 1815. During the months of his absence,
handbills had been printed showing Napoleon's face in the center
of a pansy and bearing the slogan, *Unique Pensée de la France*
(France's only thought).

Alexandre Dumas wrote in a letter: "Dear Emma, keep these two
pansies on your heart. One the colour of pain, the other the colour
of love, images of our separated and reunited hands, one is
departure, and the other return."

In *A Midsummer Night's Dream,* Shakespeare refers a great deal to
the magic power of the flower he calls "love-in-idleness" which can
"…make a man or woman madly dote/Upon the next live creature
that it sees." Oberon squeezes a pansy over Titania's eyes as she
sleeps, until a drop of its juice falls on them to have exactly the
required effect.

In the language of flowers, the pansy is not only a symbol of
remembrance but also of the power contained in a loving thought.

Pansy

Mistletoe

In 1,000 B.C., the Druids prepared infusions and potions from mistletoe as remedies against the terrible epidemics that from time to time threatened to and, to some extent did, decimate the population. Even obtaining the raw plants was a form of ceremony as the Druids used their precious bill-hooks made of gold to sever the parasitic branches which hung from the trees.

History speaks of the mistletoe harvest as of a rite that was carried out in the melancholy autumnal countryside. One can thus visualize a forest already turned red and yellow, full of lichens, moss and brambles, twisted and gnarled oak and beech trees, low shrubby undergrowth struggling to reach some light in the deep gloom – and great clusters of mistletoe attached to the branches of the trees.

Many legends about mistletoe derive from a Norwegian myth. It tells of the handsome god, Balder, made invulnerable at the behest of his mother, Frigga, who had made the whole creation promise not to harm him in any way. Balder had dreamed that he had been killed and he was anxious to tell the other gods in Valhalla; one of these gods, Loki, had hated Balder for a long time and could hardly wait for the opportunity to kill him. Disguised as an old woman, Loki asked Frigga to disclose to him whether there was any part of creation that had not sworn to protect Balder. Only the mistletoe had not been asked to give its promise because it was considered too weak and insignificant a plant and, furthermore, only grew on the edge of Valhalla. Loki went to the woods and cut down a mistletoe branch, and had another god, who was blind, throw it at Balder so that he would not be suspected at the time. Balder died instantly, but it was predicted he would eventually return to Valhalla.

In Scandinavia, mistletoe used to be gathered on the eve of the summer solstice and fires were lit during the celebrations, which were known as Balder's bonfires. The purpose of such rites was to ensure good weather, plentiful crops and protection against witchcraft. The Norwegians also believed that the life of the god was still in the mistletoe. This belief is probably due to the shape and habit of the plant, which never grows from the ground but always out of another tree and produces its berries in the winter, when everything else is in a deep sleep.

Pliny the Elder wrote in his *Historia Naturalis* that the mistletoe was also called "cure-all" by the Druids because of its medicinal properties.

Mistletoe

Wisteria

This elegant and graceful climbing plant was named wisteria in 1818, in honour of an American physician and philosopher, Casper Wistar, who was professor of Anatomy at the University of Pennsylvania. (The generic and common names are most often spelled with an "e" rather than an "a.")

This plant had arrived in England from the east coast of the United States about a hundred years before it received its official name. In the eighteenth century it was merely referred to as a "bean" or "Carolina kidney." Its great success among enthusiastic collectors was soon to spread to a much wider public, however, with the arrival from China and Japan of the splendid Asiatic species.

From the middle of the century the vines were planted in estates and gardens all over Europe, in climates ranging from cold to hot. The wisteria's adaptability to such differing temperatures and the speed with which it grows made it a favourite everywhere.

To the Chinese and Japanese, the wisteria is a symbol of tender and reciprocated friendship. It is much loved in both these countries and anyone who owns even a very small piece of land will grow one close to his house.

Japanese emperors would ensure that several wisteria plants were grown in pots in the "bonsai" method, that is, their roots and branches being kept firmly trimmed so even a plant many years old could still be held in the palm of the hand. The imperial entourage would then include a few of the best specimens – in flower, of course – among the emperor's baggage whenever he travelled around the country in the spring.

The custom then was for members of the retinue to precede the emperor, carrying the beautiful little trees. This symbolized to the hosts that the visit was being made in a spirit of goodwill, which it was assumed, was reciprocated.

Wisteria flowers contain a very sweet substance, much sought after by bees, which probably accounts for its French name, *glycine,* from the Greek *glykís,* which means "sweet."

The wisteria inspired several artists of the Art Nouveau movement who depicted them on glass, pottery, fabrics and in paintings. Lalique was particularly fond of them and used them in his exquisite work with enamel, pearls, stones and precious metals. To give a wisteria plant as a gift or to decorate a table with its blooms is an expression of friendship.

Wisteria

Calla lily

Carolus Linnaeus named this elegant white flower Calla, after the Greek word *kallós,* meaning beautiful.
The tender calla and the hardy water arum (*Calla palustris*) look very similar and therefore were included in the same genus. However, at the beginning of the nineteenth century, the German botanist, Kurt Sprengel, separated them because he discovered that they displayed some marked botanical differences.
This magnificent flower, shaped like a waxy funnel and with great purity of form, is supported on a long, sturdy stem. It received the scientific name of *Zantedeschia* in honour of Francesco Zantedeschi, an Italian physicist and botanist born in 1794.
Callas grow wild by the rivers of the Transvaal and in similar regions in the continent of Africa between the Equator and the Cape of Good Hope, forming tropical marshlands consisting of small islands. During the rainy season the underground rhizomes swell up, burst into growth and bloom, but they remain in a sort of lethargy during dry periods.
In her book, *For a Flower Album,* the French writer Colette says: "The green of the stem dilates and elongates into a horn shape. The white convolvulus that clambers among the hedgerows dilates even more and so does the long, pendulous datura, which is a poisonous jewel. But you cannot help loving the arum lily, with it excessive simplicity and its stiffness."
In the language of flowers the calla lilies are linked to beauty.

Calla lily

Zinnia

The credit for classifying this plant goes to Carolus Linnaeus, the Swedish doctor and scientist as well as one of the most outstanding botanists in the world. He was born in Raashult in 1707 and died in 1778. He was the son of a peasant and studied medicine and botany, later teaching both at the University of Uppsala.

His botany professor was quite taken aback when his favourite pupil, then aged twenty-three, presented a paper on plant reproduction in the form of an operetta. In the same year, 1730, Linnaeus was invited to give a course of lectures on his scientific research to date and this led him to specialize in botany as his life's work. Before long, the young scientist became only too aware of the inadequacies of the many plant classification systems then in existence. Most of them consisted of long names and confusing descriptions. Although a haphazard binomial system had been used, in 1753 Linnaeus introduced his system, which named and described plants according to genus and species, giving two Latin names to every type of plant – and later, he extended the system to all living things on earth, including himself. The first name was a noun that would describe the genus and the second, an adjective or adjectival noun that would denote the species. With his amazing capacity for observation, Linnaeus had refined and devised a system of classification that still remains the basis for modern plant nomenclature.

In order to find suitable names for plants, this enterprising botanist often used the names of plant hunters, explorers and scholars whom he believed deserved such recognition.

He dedicated a plant that had arrived in England from Mexico, where it is particularly widely distributed, to Gottfried Zinn, one of his disciples. The plant was *Zinnia elegans,* the major parent of today's many zinnia varieties. A few other zinnia species are indigenous to Colorado, New Mexico, Kansas, Arizona and Texas as well as the Argentine in South America. By the second half of the eighteenth century, most of these species had reached Europe. Along with *Z. elegans,* these and other species were used to create the zinnia hybrids we grow today in our gardens.

There is nothing pompous about the cheerful zinnia. Perhaps because of this – and the fact that it is easy to grow – the meaning that has been given to it in the language of flowers is simplicity. The zinnia can therefore be regarded as the most appropriate flower with which to express admiration when faced with genuine artlessness and lack of pretension.

Zinnia

Appendix

Acacia and Mimosa (Sensitive Plant)
Acacia decurrens (1)
Acacia farnesiana (2)
Mimosa pudica (3)

FAMILY *Leguminosae*.
PLACE OF ORIGIN Australia, Tasmania (*A. decurrens*); tropical America (*A. farnesiana*); tropical America (*M. pudica*).
TYPE OF PLANT Trees or shrubs, evergreen or deciduous, the leaves having divided lobes. The branches of *M. pudica*, the sensitive plant, die after flowering; it is very dainty and is usually grown as an annual. Its leaves close up if touched. *A. decurrens* (and a similar species, *A. dealbata*) is the typical mimosa sold by florists as cut flowers.
HEIGHT 2-3 m (6½-10 ft) (*A. farnesiana*); 10-25 m (33-82 ft) (*A. decurrens*); 0.5-1.5 m (1½-3 ft) (*M. pudica*).
SOIL TYPE Slightly acid.
MOISTURE Frequent watering when in bloom.
POSITION Sunny and sheltered; semi-shade, in hot areas, for *M. pudica*.
CLIMATE Warm temperate to tropical as on the Mediterranean coasts and lakes and in southern California.
PROPAGATION By seed in spring or by cuttings; *M. pudica* by seed any time – indoors in winter, outside in summer.
TRANSPLANTING TIME Autumn–spring.
FLOWERING TIME Mostly late winter to spring. The flowers of Acacia species consist of small, yellow global heads, highly scented. *M. pudica* blooms with pink heads in summer – autumn.
USES As ornamental plants in gardens and in the North as greenhouse and conservatory subjects; also as a cut flower.
CUTTING BACK This usually occurs with acacias when the flowers are gathered. If necessary, any branches that spoil the shape of the tree or shrub should be cut out.
DISEASES Root rot, branch canker and chlorosis on soil that contains too much lime.

Acacia
Acacia floribunda (syn. *Acacia retinodes*)

FAMILY *Leguminosae*.
PLACE OF ORIGIN Australia.
TYPE OF PLANT Small tree or hardy shrub whose leaves are replaced by leaflike petioles called phyllodes when the flowers appear.
HEIGHT 5-6 m (16½-20 ft).
SOIL TYPE Fertile, moist but well drained, preferably slightly acid or neutral.
MOISTURE Regular watering; abundant watering when flowering.
POSITION Sunny.
CLIMATE Warm temperate to tropical.
PROPAGATION By seed in spring or by cuttings.
TRANSPLANTING TIME Autumn–spring.
FLOWERING TIME The whole summer. Its fluffy flowers are yellow and grow in clusters.
USES Suitable for the garden in warm climates and for growing in large pots or tubs on a terrace, patio or balcony and in the North in greenhouses.
DISEASES Root rot and branch canker.

Acanthus
Acanthus mollis

FAMILY *Acanthaceae*.
PLACE OF ORIGIN Mediterranean Europe.
TYPE OF PLANT Herbaceous perennial; it has large, very decorative, glossy lobed leaves with a wavy edge. Because of its large size, the most widespread variety is *Acanthus mollis latifolius*. This plant is also known as bear's breech.
HEIGHT 60-90 cm (24-36 ins).
SOIL TYPE Deep, well worked and moist with good drainage.
MOISTURE Regular watering.
POSITION Sunny or slightly shaded.
CLIMATE Temperate-cool; fairly frost-resistant but not reliably winter-hardy in North.
PROPAGATION By seed in spring or by clump division in the autumn or spring or root cuttings in early spring.
TRANSPLANTING TIME Autumn–spring.
FLOWERING TIME Summer. The flower heads consist of long spikes of white flowers with purple veins.
USES In flower borders or large pots or tubs on the terrace. When dried, the flower spikes make an attractive contribution to flower arrangements.
CUTTING BACK The stems should be cut down to ground level after flowering.
DISEASES Black spot.

Aconite
Aconitum napellus

FAMILY *Ranunculaceae*.
PLACE OF ORIGIN Europe, Asia.
TYPE OF PLANT Herbaceous perennial, hardy, with dark green leaves cut deeply at the margin. Monkshood is a very poisonous plant.
HEIGHT Up to 1.2 m (4 ft).
SOIL TYPE Fertile and humus-rich (mix in peat moss).
MOISTURE Frequent watering; at least once a day in dry weather.
POSITION Semi-shade, but sun-tolerant in moisture-retaining soil.
CLIMATE Temperate.
PROPAGATION By seed in the spring or by division of the tubers in the spring or autumn.
TRANSPLANTING TIME Early spring or autumn.
FLOWERING TIME Summer. Dark violet-blue flowers – but other species and varieties are light blue, white, or variegated – borne in succession up the main stem.
USES In flowerbeds and rock gardens. As a medicinal plant, a fluid extract and a tincture for external use can be made from the dried tubers and leaves.
CUTTING BACK All stems should be cut back after flowering in the autumn.

Amaranth
Amaranthus caudatus

FAMILY *Amaranthaceaea*.
PLACE OF ORIGIN The tropics.
TYPE OF PLANT Herbaceous annual, well branched, with light green, heart-shaped leaves, that are edible when young. Also known as love-lies-bleeding.
HEIGHT 1-1.5m (3¼-5ft).
SOIL TYPE Deep, well fertilized.
MOISTURE Regular watering.
POSITION Sunny.
CLIMATE Temperate.
PROPAGATION By seed in the spring.
TRANSPLANTING TIME Late spring.
FLOWERING TIME Summer. The long red or greenish spikes are pendulous and, if picked, will last until the autumn.
USES To give a little height in a border and as a pot-plant.
PESTS Aphids.
DISEASES White rust.

Poppy Anemone
Anemone coronaria

FAMILY *Ranunculaceae*.
PLACE OF ORIGIN Eastern Mediterranean.
TYPE OF PLANT Herbaceous perennial, deciduous, with a branched rhizome and deeply cut lobed leaves.
HEIGHT 15-30cm (6-12ins).
SOIL TYPE Any type, fertile, well drained, not too dry.
MOISTURE Regular watering.
POSITION Sunny or in semi-shade.
CLIMATE Temperate; in the colder areas it is a good idea to protect the rhizomes with leaves during the winter.
PROPAGATION By separating the side shoots. By dividing the rhizomes in autumn or in the spring. By seed in the spring.
TRANSPLANTING TIME Autumn.
FLOWERING TIME Early spring. Its flowers may be white, red, violet-blue or pink, according to the variety.
USES In borders or rock gardens; as a pot plant or as cut flowers.
PESTS Aphids and nematodes.
DISEASEAS Rust, downy mildew, crown and rhizome rot and botrytis blight.

Snapdragon
Antirrhinum majus

FAMILY *Scrophulariaceae*.
PLACE OF ORIGIN Italy and other Mediterranean regions.
TYPE OF PLANT Perennial, hardy, but usually grown as an annual. Stems woody at the base. Dark green, flattened leaves shaped like lance heads.
HEIGHT 30-100 cm (12-40 ins), depending on the variety which may be dwarf, medium or tall.
SOIL TYPE Any well drained type, but sandy soils require addition of organic matter and fertilizer.
MOISTURE Regular watering as needed; more frequent during dry weather in the summer.
POSITION In full sun.
CLIMATE Temperate; protect during the winter in cold areas where it is usually regarded as a biennial.
PROPAGATION By seed sown indoors in early spring; in mild winter areas, by seed in autumn for flowering the following spring and summer.
TRANSPLANTING TIME In the autumn or spring, depending on the climate.
FLOWERING TIME From summer to autumn if fading flowers are removed. The flower spikes range in colour from white to yellow, scarlet, deep red and purple. The flowers are fragrant.
USES In borders, flowerbeds, decorative containers, troughs and window-boxes. The larger varieties are excellent as cut flowers.
CUTTING BACK The tops of young plants should be pinched off to encourage a bushy growth and all dead flowers cut off to prolong the flowering period.
PESTS Aphids.
DISEASES Rootrot, moulds and rust, but the latter can be avoided by buying rust-resistant strains.

Aquilegia or Columbine
Aquilegia vulgaris (1)
Aquilegia vulgaris hybrids (2-3)

FAMILY *Ranunculaceae*.
PLACE OF ORIGIN Europe.
TYPE OF PLANT Herbaceous perennial, hardy. Forms strong clumps and flowers freely in the spring. Also known as European crowfoot.
HEIGHT Up to 10-30 cm to 40-90 cm (4-12 ins to 16-36 ins), according to the variety.
SOIL TYPE Light, moist, loamy (add humus to sandy soils), preferably acid or neutral.
MOISTURE Well drained soil or the fleshy roots will rot.
POSITION Sun, or semi-shade.
CLIMATE Winter-hardy in the North. Prefers cool rather than hot summers.
PROPAGATION By seed in spring or summer. By clump division in spring but renewing stock by seeds is more reliable.
TRANSPLANTING TIME Autumn or early spring for established plants; seedlings from spring to autumn.
FLOWERING TIME May-June. The flowers vary in colour from violet to white and red-purple.
USES In herbaceous borders and beds; also rock gardens. Plants grow well in pots, tubs and troughs for a time.
CUTTING BACK The taller varieties should be cut back to ground level after flowering.
PESTS Aphids and leafminers that make unsightly irregular tunnels in the leaves.
DISEASES Rust, a fungus leaf spot and crown or root rot.

Arbutus or Strawberry tree
Arbutus unedo

FAMILY *Ericaceae*.
PLACE OF ORIGIN Southern Europe and Ireland.
TYPE OF PLANT Small evergreen tree or shrub, with dark green, glossy leaves; it is typical of the Mediterranean *maquis*.
HEIGHT From 4-6m (13-20ft), occasionally reaching 10m (33ft).
SOIL TYPE Slightly acid, humus-rich.
POSITION Sunny and sheltered from cold winds.
CLIMATE Hardy in the Pacific Northwest and as far north as Georgia on East Coast.
PROPAGATION By seed in the spring, cuttings in the autumn, or by grafting in summer.
TRANSPLANTING TIME Autumn or spring.
FLOWERING TIME Autumn to early winter. Its white flowers hang down in small clusters. Flowering occurs at the same time as the fruit ripens to an orangey-red colour.
USES It is grown as a decorative shrub or tree for its beautiful foliage and the redness of its fruit, which is edible but soon devoured by birds; it is also suitable for terraces and patios, when grown in a large container.
CUTTING BACK Its slow growth makes this unnecessary; if it throws up too many shoots they can be thinned out.

Asphodel
Asphodelus cerasiferus (syn. *A. ramosus*)

FAMILY *Liliaceae.*
PLACE OF ORIGIN Europe, western Asia.
TYPE OF PLANT Hardy herbaceous, perennial, with clumps of long, slender, deciduous leaves. Also known as silver rod.
HEIGHT 50-150cm (20-60ins).
SOIL TYPE Ordinary garden soil, of any type.
MOISTURE Should not be watered a great deal.
POSITION Sunny or partially shaded.
CLIMATE Temperate-mild; in colder areas the plants should be protected during the winter.
PROPAGATION By division of the tuberous roots in autumn or spring, or seeds sown in spring.
TRANSPLANTING TIME Autumn or spring.
FLOWERING TIME Summer. The white or pale pink flowers are clustered along the top of the stalk.
USES Flowerbeds and borders.

Aster
Aster novi-belgii

FAMILY *Compositae.*
PLACE OF ORIGIN North America.
TYPE OF PLANT Herbaceous perennial; it has an erect, expansive habit and whole or tooth-edged lance-head-shaped leaves. This species is known as New York aster and is an important parent of the hybrids known as Michaelmas asters.
HEIGHT 1.2-1.5 m (4-5 ft), according to the variety.
SOIL TYPE Any type, well drained.
MOISTURE Abundant watering before and during flowering period.
POSITION Sunny.
CLIMATE Temperate-cool; very hardy.
PROPAGATION By clump division in the spring, usually every year or so to keep the plants vigorous.
TRANSPLANTING TIME Autumn or spring.
FLOWERING TIME Summer to autumn, according to the variety. The heads are of different sizes with daisy flowers, single or double. The species has blue flowers but most garden asters are hybrids with a colour range from white to pink and crimson, and from light blue to a deep violet-blue, usually with a yellow center.
USES Ideal for borders, especially in combination with chrysanthemums.
CUTTING BACK In late autumn when flowering ends, the clumps should be cut down to ground level.
PESTS Rabbits will eat new spring growth.
DISEASES Root rot and mildew.

Daisy
Bellis perennis (1)
Bellis perennis "Monstrosa" (2)
Chrysanthemum leucanthemum (3)

FAMILY *Compositae.*
PLACE OF ORIGIN Europe, Asia Minor.
TYPE OF PLANT English daisies (*Bellis perennis*) are hardy biennials or perennials. They are the wild, low-growing daisies of Europe and the British Isles, which are charming but regarded as a nuisance when they self-sow in well kept lawns. The oxeye daisy (*Chrysanthemum leucanthemum*), a hardy perennial, grows like a native plant in the USA and is common in fields and along roads.
HEIGHT 10-15 cm (4-6 ins), according to the variety, for *B. perennis*; up to 40-60 cm (16-24 ins) for *C. leucanthemum*.
SOIL TYPE Ordinary to fertile garden soil.
MOISTURE Average watering as necessary.
POSITION Full sun or light shade.
CLIMATE Temperate.
PROPAGATION By clump division after flowering for oxeye daisy. By seed in early summer for English daisies.
TRANSPLANTING TIME Autumn or spring.
FLOWERING TIME Spring for English daisies. Their heads are white, sometimes tinged with pink, with a yellow center. The double and semi-double garden varieties range in colour from white to pink, red and crimson. The oxeye daisy blooms from late spring to midsummer. Its flowers are white.
USES Borders and flowerbeds; they also grow well in pots or tubs on patios, terraces.
DISEASES Grey mould (botrytis), common on English daisies in humid, overcast weather.

Calendula or Pot marigold
Calendula officinalis

FAMILY *Compositae.*
PLACE OF ORIGIN Southern Europe.
TYPE OF PLANT Herbaceous annual. Bushy habit. Its light green leaves are oval and soft.
HEIGHT Up to 40-60 cm (16-24 ins).
SOIL TYPE Garden soil, even if poor, but good drainage essential.
MOISTURE Abundant watering.
POSITION Sunny.
CLIMATE Temperate. Plants can be sown in the autumn in mild winter regions. Elsewhere, seeds should be sown in early spring as garden varieties do not thrive in hot summer weather.
PROPAGATION By seed in September or spring.
TRANSPLANTING TIME Spring.
FLOWERING TIME Early summer to autumn in cool summer regions. The flowers are bright orange but colours range from cream to yellow and deep orange, especially in the double varieties, such as the "Pacific Hybrids."
USES Borders and flowerbeds; they grow well in pots, tubs and window-boxes.
CUTTING BACK Pinch out the main shoots and remove fading flowers regularly to encourage flowering.
PESTS Aphids.
DISEASES Mildew, leaf spot and rust.

Camellia
Camellia japonica

FAMILY *Theaceae.*
PLACE OF ORIGIN Japan, China, southern Korea.
TYPE OF PLANT Tree or shrub, evergreen.
HEIGHT Up to 3-7 m (10-23 ft), according to the variety; slow growing.
SOIL TYPE Acid, rich in organic materials, well drained, damp.
MOISTURE Abundant watering; the leaves should be sprayed in the summer when the atmosphere is very dry.
POSITION Shaded or semi-shaded; sheltered from the wind, as this plant is easily damaged by cold, hot or dry winds.
CLIMATE Temperate-humid; tolerant to cold down to −5°C (23°F), but not reliably hardy in northern regions. Thrives in Southeast and Pacific Coast areas of USA.
PROPAGATION By cuttings, layering and grafting in the summer. By seed – but growth is very slow.
TRANSPLANTING TIME Autumn or late winter to early spring, depending on climate.
FLOWERING TIME Late winter to spring. The flowers can be single, double or semi-double and white, pink or a rich red, often variegated according to the variety.
USES As isolated plants or forming a hedge. An individual flower makes an excellent boutonniere. Suitable for pots and tubs on terraces, patios, or in greenhouses.
CUTTING BACK Dead branches should be trimmed back after flowering and a light pruning given to retain the shape of the plant as necessary.
PESTS Aphids, mealybugs, and, especially, scale insects.
DISEASES Distorted leaves are usually caused by frost; dark patches on the leaves may due be to lime in the soil.

Bignonia Trumpet vine
*Campsis radicans (*syn. *Bignonia radicans, Tecoma radicans)*

FAMILY *Bignoniaceae.*
PLACE OF ORIGIN Southeastern United States.
TYPE OF PLANT Climbing shrub with deciduous compound leaves, the leaflets arranged in pairs with a single one at the end of each group. It produces numerous aerial roots to cling to its supports.
HEIGHT Up to 12m (40ft).
SOIL TYPE Ordinary, well drained garden soil.
MOISTURE In dry weather, water once a week.
POSITION Sun.
CLIMATE Very hardy, to −20°C (−4°F).
PROPAGATION By cuttings in the spring or late summer. By layering in the autumn. By seed in spring.
TRANSPLANTING TIME Autumn or early spring.
FLOWERING TIME Summer-autumn. The flowers are deep orange and shaped like small trumpets.
USES An exellent cover for walls, fences, pergolas, trellises. It also grows well in tubs or large pots on terraces, patios, providing it has supports to cling to.
CUTTING BACK after planting, it should be cut to little more than 20cm (8ins) from the ground to encourage the new shoots. Thereafter, cut back in early spring as needed.
PESTS Almost insect proof.

Cornflower
Centaurea cyanus

FAMILY *Compositae.*
PLACE OF ORIGIN Europe; similar species from Eastern Asia and Asia Minor.
TYPE OF PLANT Herbaceous annual, with an erect, well branched stem. In mild winter regions can be grown as biennial.
HEIGHT 30-80cm (12-32 ins), according to the variety.
SOIL TYPE Not particularly rich. The hardy perennial species such as *C.dealbata* and *C.montana*, prefer dry, stony places.
MOISTURE Regular watering during drought.
POSITION Sun.
CLIMATE Temperate; cool summer conditions prolong flowering.
PROPAGATION By seed in spring; autumn in mild climates.
TRANSPLANTING TIME Spring.
FLOWERING TIME Usually early summer. The plants peter out in hot weather. Each spray bears several bright blue flowers in the typical species; in the garden varieties, the flowers are larger and colours include white, pink and reddish-pink.
USES For borders and flowerbeds; they grow well in pots for a time and are good for cutting.
CUTTING BACK Remove fading flowers regularly to prolong flowering time.
DISEASES Mildew.

Wallflower
Cheiranthus cheiri

FAMILY *Cruciferae*.
PLACE OF ORIGIN Europe.
TYPE OF PLANT Herbaceous perennial but grown as a biennial, with an erect habit; its deciduous, dark green leaves are shaped like lance heads.
HEIGHT 30-60 cm (12-24 ins), according to the variety which can be dwarf or of bedding height.
SOIL TYPE Well drained, slightly limy (alkaline) garden soil of any type.
MOISTURE Regular watering.
POSITION Sunny or semi-shaded.
CLIMATE Temperate; the young plants should be protected by a mulch where the winter is very cold.
PROPAGATION By seed in early summer.
TRANSPLANTING TIME Autumn or early spring.
FLOWERING TIME Spring. The flowers, very fragrant, form clusters along the top of the stems. Colours vary through yellow, orange, brown, red, salmon pink, crimson, white, purple and even variegated.
USES For borders, flowerbeds and rock gardens. They combine well with tulips and particularly well in new or old stone walls as well as in pots, tubs.
CUTTING BACK Pinch out the tops when the plants are 10-15 cm (4-6 ins) high to encourage each plant to bush out.
PESTS Root aphids and cabbage white caterpillars.
DISEASES Clubroot, grey mould (botrytis).

Greater Celandine
Chelidonium majus

FAMILY *Papaveraceae*.
PLACE OF ORIGIN Europe.
TYPE OF PLANT Perennial, with well-branched stem. It can be an intrusive weed.
HEIGHT 30-100 cm (12-40 ins).
SOIL TYPE Rich in leafmould and humus-like materials.
MOISTURE It grows even in damp places.
POSITION Sunny or semi-shaded.
PROPOGATION By seed.
FLOWERING TIME Mostly spring; its little flowers are golden yellow.
USES Another European native that has escaped from cultivation in the USA. It grows wild on walls, by the roadside and at the edges of woods. It exudes a form of yellow latex, when the stems are cut, which has medicinal properties.

Wintersweet
Chimonanthus praecox

FAMILY *Calycanthaceae*
PLACE OF ORIGIN China.
TYPE OF PLANT Deciduous, well-branched shrub with lance head shaped leaves.
HEIGHT Up to 2-3m (7-10ft).
SOIL TYPE Any type of moist garden soil.
MOISTURE Weekly watering in spring and autumn, more frequently in summer.
POSITION Sunny and sheltered. Cold winds are harmful.
CLIMATE Temperate. Not hardy where temperatures fall – and remain long – below −12°C (10°F).
PROPAGATION By seed or layering in early autumn. Alternatively, the basal shoots can be removed in spring or autumn and planted immediately.
TRANSPLANTING TIME Spring or autumn.
FLOWERING TIME Midwinter to spring. The flowers, which emerge on the bare base branches, are small and sweetly scented; they are yellow on the outside and purple on the inside.
USES For the winter garden in mild winter regions. Also for cutting.
CUTTING BACK The branches should be thinned out after flowering as necessary.

Chrysanthemum
Chrysanthemum × morifolium
(syn. *Chrysanthemum × hortorum*)

FAMILY *Compositae.*
PLACE OF ORIGIN Mediterranean basin, the Caucasus, China, Korea, Canary Islands.
TYPE OF PLANT Mostly hardy, herbaceous or semi-shrubby perennials, sometimes evergreen in mild winter regions. Erect or prostrate habit, according to the variety.
HEIGHT 30-150cm (12-60 ins).
SOIL TYPE Any type of open, well drained soil, that retains moisture.
MOISTURE Should be kept constant with regular watering, as needed.
POSITION Sunny and sheltered.
CLIMATE Temperate.
PROPAGATION By cuttings or clump division.
FLOWERING TIME Mostly late summer to autumn. Colours of the flowers include yellow, white, pink, purple, bronze and crimson; they vary widely in size and shape, according to the variety, and may be single or double. They are very long lasting, either on the plant or when cut for arrangements.
USES Suitable for borders, flowerbeds, tubs and pots. It is an excellent flower for cutting.
CUTTING BACK The plants are cut back in spring and shoots pinched back again in early summer. Disbudding is practical on large – flowered "football" types and other varieties to achieve one huge flower per stem.
PESTS Earwigs in the flowers, cutworms and snails in spring.
DISEASES Viruses, mildew, rust and rotting of the floral buds and stems.

Citron
Citrus medica

FAMILY *Rutaceae.*
PLACE OF ORIGIN India.
TYPE OF PLANT Spiny, evergreen tree with bright green, oval leaves.
HEIGHT 3-4 m (10-13 ft).
SOIL TYPE Open and rich in organic materials.
MOISTURE Abundant watering, especially for plants grown in pots, tubs.
POSITION Sunny and sheltered.
CLIMATE Temperate-hot and dry. In the USA, grown in Florida and California. In cooler climes, citron trees can be grown in large pots and brought into a well lighted plant room or greenhouse in the winter where the frosts cannot reach them.
PROPAGATION By seed in the spring and by cuttings and grafting.
FLOWERING TIME All the year. The sweetly-scented flowers are white and tinged with violet on the outside. Its fruit is like a lemon but larger.
USES As a fruit and decorative tree in gardens; adapts well to cultivation in tubs, large pots.
CUTTING BACK Reduce the head of any plants grown in pots, tubs, by shortening the branches to one half of their original length every 2-3 years.
PESTS Aphids and scale insects.

Orange
Citrus sinensis

FAMILY *Rutaceae.*
PLACE OF ORIGIN China.
TYPE OF PLANT Evergreen tree, sometimes spiny, with a roundish head; its oval leaves are bright green.
HEIGHT Up to 8 m (approx. 26 ft).
SOIL TYPE Open, well drained and enriched with organic matter.
MOISTURE Abundant watering; especially for plants in tubs, pots.
POSITION Sunny.
CLIMATE Temperate-hot and dry. In the North, orange trees can be grown in large pots and brought into a well lighted position in a plant room or greenhouse in the winter where the frosts cannot reach them.
PROPAGATION By seed in the spring or anytime indoors and by grafting.
TRANSPLANTING TIME Mostly spring to early summer.
FLOWERING TIME Spring, but some blooms appear all year. The white flowers are very sweetly scented. Plants may fruit and flower at the same time.
USES As a fruit and ornamental tree in gardens; adapts well to cultivation in tubs, large pots.
CUTTING BACK Remove old branches and trim to keep the rounded shape of the head.
PESTS Aphids, mealybugs, whiteflies and scale insects.

Clematis
Clematis alpina (1)
Clematis hybrids (2)
Clematis vitalba (3)

FAMILY *Ranunculaceae.*
PLACE OF ORIGIN Central and southern Europe, northern Asia for *C. alpina;* Europe for *C. vitalba.* The hybrids, many of which may be over 100 years old, are derived from these and many other species, native to Asia and North America.
TYPE OF PLANT Mostly climbing, woody vines, clinging to supports by tendril-like leaves. Some species, such as the invasive *C. vitalba,* are very robust, while its relative, *C. alpina,* is slow growing and compact. The hybrids vary according to the vigour of their parents.
HEIGHT Up to 1.8-12 m (6-40 ft).
SOIL TYPE Limy garden soil, deep and well drained.
MOISTURE Frequent watering, every day at the hottest time of the year. Keep ground moist.
POSITION Sunny or half-shade. Most vines, especially the hybrids, prefer to have their roots in the shade; when grown in a tub or pot this must be roomy and partially shaded.
CLIMATE Temperate.
PROPAGATION By cuttings in summer and by seed in spring. Also by division and layers.
TRANSPLANTING TIME Early spring or autumn.
FLOWERING TIME Summer, with small ivory flowers (*C. vitalba*); spring, bell like, drooping, light blue-violet flowers (*C. alpina*); mostly summer, flat, open flowers ranging through light blue, blue-violet, dark purple-violet, pink, red, white (*Clematis hybrids*).
USES Covering plant for trellises and walls.
CUTTING BACK Prune according to whether the vines bloom on old or new wood. New wood: prune in early spring; old wood: prune after flowering.
PESTS Aphids and earwigs in the flowers.
DISEASES Die-back, mildew, and leaf spot.

Lily of the valley
Convallaria majalis

FAMILY *Liliaceae.*
PLACE OF ORIGIN Europe, Asia, North America.
TYPE OF PLANT Herbaceous perennial, deciduous, hardy with a rhizomatous root that branches out sideways. Its light green leaves are lance head shaped, growing upwards.
HEIGHT 20 cm (8 ins).
SOIL TYPE Any type of soil, preferably enriched with leafmould and/or peat moss and well-drained.
MOISTURE Regular watering until the flowering period, when it should be reduced.
POSITION Shady or semi-shady.
CLIMATE Temperate-cool.
PROPAGATION By rhizome division in spring or autumn. By seed in autumn, but division is faster.
TRANSPLANTING TIME Right after flowering or in autumn.
FLOWERING TIME Spring. The white, bell-shaped flowers are sweetly scented and arranged singly up one side of the top third of the stem.
USES In borders, although the ideal position is in the shade of deciduous trees and shrubs as a ground cover. The lily of the valley also grows well in pots for a time.
PESTS Nematodes.
DISEASES Grey mould, rust and leaf spot.

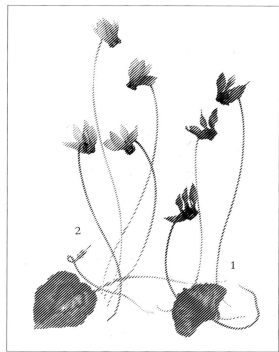

Crocus
Crocus vernus

FAMILY *Iridaceae*
PLACE OF ORIGIN Italy, Asia.
TYPE OF PLANT Cormous, hardy perennial, with very narrow, ribbon-like leaves which grow upwards and die back after flowering.
SOIL TYPE Well drained and rich.
MOISTURE A little water if exceptionally dry; usually there is no need to water for spring-blooming kinds.
POSITION Sunny or slightly shady.
CLIMATE Temperate.
PROPAGATION By separation of the cormels in the summer, when the leaves are brown. Plants often self-sow.
TRANSPLANTING TIME From summer to early autumn. New corms are available from dealers in autumn for garden planting or for pots for indoor forcing.
FLOWERING TIME Spring. Colours range through white, violet, lilac, purple, dark blue and yellow. Forced plants will bloom indoors from Christmas through spring.
USES As an attractive early spring bedding bulb; excellent, too, when scattered in lawns, also in pots, tubs or window boxes.
CUTTING BACK Allow the leaves and flowers to die off completely. Green foliage must not be mowed in lawns if plants are to bloom the next spring.
PESTS Mice, squirrels.
DISEASES Various bulb rots.

Cyclamen
Cyclamen europaeum (1) (syn. *C. purpurascens*).
Cyclamen neapolitanum (2) (syn. *C. hederifolium*).

FAMILY *Primulaceae*.
PLACE OF ORIGIN Central and southern Europe (*C. europaeum*) Italy, Greece (*C. neapolitanum*).
TYPE OF PLANT Herbaceous perennial, cormous; heart-shaped, dark green leaves with lighter markings, often dark red on their undersides.
HEIGHT 10 cm (4 ins) *C. europaeum;* 15-20 cm (6-8 ins) *C. neapolitanum.*
SOIL TYPE Well drained and organically rich.
MOISTURE Abundant and frequent watering unless dormant; cyclamens thrive in a damp environment.
POSITION Shady or semi-shady.
CLIMATE Temperate; being indigenous to Italy, the *C. neapolitanum* grows prolifically in many parts of that country. Not reliably hardy in the North. Dealers usually ship corms in early autumn.
PROPAGATION Only by seed, in spring.
TRANSPLANTING TIME After flowering, the resting period for the corms.
FLOWERING TIME Late summer: the sweetly scented flowers of *C. europaeum* are carmine red. Autumn: the flowers of *C. neapolitanum* are mauve.
USES Under bushes and shrubs or any shady spot; rock gardens; suitable for pots, tubs.
PESTS Mites and aphids which damage the leaves; mice, which eat the corms.
DISEASES Grey mould.

Dahlia
Dahila pinnata (syn. *D. variablis*)

FAMILY *Compositae*.
PLACE OF ORIGIN Mexico.
TYPE OF PLANT Herbaceous, tuberous perennial, with a bushy habit.
HEIGHT From 25-50 cm up to 2.5 m (10-12 ins up to 8½ ft).
SOIL TYPE Ordinary, well drained garden soil.
MOISTURE Abundant watering during any hot summer weather.
POSITION Sunny and open.
CLIMATE Temperate. Any recently planted tubers should be sheltered from frost in the colder areas.
PROPAGATION By tuber division in early spring. By seed in the spring.
TRANSPLANTING TIME Spring and autumn when the tubers must be dug and stored in a frost-free room or cellar.
FLOWERING TIME Late summer–autumn. The flowers range through white, yellow, red, pink, purple, mauve and striped; they may be large or small, single or double and of various forms.
USES Borders and flowerbeds; the smaller varieties grow well in pots and all are good for picking. The taller border varieties as well as the very large-flowered kinds grown for exhibitions need to be staked.
CUTTING BACK The top of the main shoot should be pinched out of the border varieties, about a month after they have been planted out in the spring.
PESTS Aphids, red spider mites and earwigs in the flowers.
DISEASES Grey mould, root rot and wet rot in the cuttings.

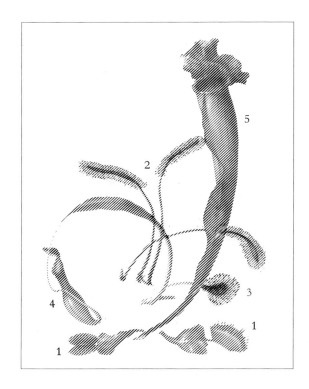

Datura
Datura stramonium

FAMILY *Solanaceae*.
PLACE OF ORIGIN Western Asia, Italy.
TYPE OF PLANT Herbaceous, short-lived perennial or annual, well branched, with dark green, oval leaves splaying out into points at each side and at the tip.
HEIGHT Up to 1.5 m (5 ft).
SOIL TYPE Ordinary garden soil. Tolerant of varying soils.
MOISTURE Generous watering during hot spells.
POSITION Sunny.
CLIMATE Mild or warm coastal atmosphere.
PROPAGATION By seed indoors in early spring, or sown outdoors when soil has warmed.
TRANSPLANTING TIME Usually late spring.
FLOWERING TIME Summer. The flowers are white and shaped like large elongated bells.
USES A large plant for the back of herbaceous borders. This plant grows well in large pots or tubs on terraces, patios.
PESTS Red spider mites, which damage the leaves.

Carnation
Dianthus caryophyllus

FAMILY *Caryophyllaceae*.
PLACE OF ORIGIN South-west Europe.
TYPE OF PLANT Perennial, evergreen, with silvery-green, lance head shaped leaves, usually grown as an annual.
HEIGHT 30 cm-1 m (12-40 ins).
SOIL TYPE Friable, slightly limy (alkaline) garden soil.
MOISTURE Regular watering; the soil should not be allowed to become bone dry.
POSITION Sunny.
CLIMATE Temperate; if the weather is mild, flowering may continue into late fall.
PROPAGATION By seed indoors in late winter. By cuttings in summer.
TRANSPLANTING TIME Spring or autumn.
FLOWERING TIME Summer. The flowers may be one-coloured or variegated. They do not thrive where summers are very hot.
USES Borders, rock gardens, in pots or as cut flowers. Also in greenhouses for winter bloom.
CUTTING BACK Cut the stems right back to base after flowering. Pinch out the tops in spring to obtain more buds for summer.
PESTS Aphids, red spiders.
DISEASES Root rot among cuttings, leaf spot and rust. Greenhouse plants are susceptible to many diseases.

Carnivorous plants
Dionaea muscipula (1).
Drosera capensis (2).
Drosera rotundifolia (3)
Sarracenia alata (4)
Sarracenia chelsonii (5)

FAMILY *Sarraceniaceae: S.alata, S. x chelsonii; Droseraceae: D.muscipula, D.capensis, D.rotundifolia*.
PLACE OF ORIGIN North America: *S.alata, S. x chelsonii, D.rotundifolia:* coastal South and North Carolina; Asia, South Africa: *D.capensis*.
TYPE OF PLANT Herbaceous perennial, rhizomatous or tufted, usually evergreen. The leaves of *D.muscipula* unite in a tuft and are formed into a two-lobed sheath with sensitive edges; any insects that land on their surface are captured by closing the two lobes. *S.alata* and *S.chelsonii* have elongated leaves and cavities shaped rather like goblets, containing a liquid to attract the insects, which then drown. The *Drosera* have long-stemmed, spatula-shaped leaves; they are viscous and covered with reddish hairs.
HEIGHT 10-15 cm (4-6 ins) and 76.2 cm (30 in) or so for pitcher plants.
SOIL TYPE Peaty, acid, moist.
MOISTURE Watering and spraying every day during the summer. These are bog plants and can not be grown under usual garden conditions.
POSITION Sun or light shade.
CLIMATE Some of these plants are quite hardy. Others are native to the tropics.
PROPAGATION By seed in spring, (*S.alata, S.chelsonii*) and in the autumn (*D.muscipula, Drosera*). Separation of the rhizomes in the spring is the easier method.
TRANSPLANTING TIME Late winter.
FLOWERING TIME Spring to autumn.
USES In pots as ornamental – and rather strange – plants in a greenhouse or in a bog garden outdoors.

Freesia
Freesia x hybrida

FAMILY *Iridaceae.*
PLACE OF ORIGIN Southern Africa.
TYPE OF PLANT Tender, bulbous perennial, with deciduous, ribbon-like leaves.
HEIGHT Up to 50-60 cm (20-24 ins).
SOIL TYPE Fertile and light.
MOISTURE Abundant watering as the plants come into flower, decreasing as the flowers fade, then allowed to dry out completely.
POSITION Sunny and sheltered.
CLIMATE Mild. In cold areas the bulbs must be grown in the winter in a cool but frost-free atmosphere, such as a sunny window or in a greenhouse.
PROPAGATION By seed or by separation after foliage has died down. Usual and quicker method is to buy bulbs in autumn.
TRANSPLANTING TIME In cold areas the bulbs should be planted in autumn in pots for indoor flowering. In mild areas, they can be planted out in autumn and left in the ground for several years.
FLOWERING TIME Usually winter to spring. These sweetly scented flowers are arranged along one side of the top of each stem, their colours ranging from white to various shades of yellow, white, violet and red.
USES Mainly as cut flowers.
PESTS Stems and leaves are prone to infestations of aphids and red spiders.

Fuchsia
Fuchsia hybrids

FAMILY *Onagraceae.*
PLACE OF ORIGIN Central and South America, New Zealand.
TYPE OF PLANT Small, evergreen (in mild climates) tree or shrub with an erect or prostrate habit. Its lance head shaped leaves are green tinged with a violet-reddish colour.
HEIGHT 1-3 m (3-10 ft).
SOIL TYPE Organic, rich, lime-free, well drained.
MOISTURE This should be kept constant (except during winter rest) with regular watering, especially with potted plants.
POSITION Semi-shade or full-shade but light and airy.
CLIMATE Mild-cool; in cold climates the plants usually in containers, should be cut back and stored in darkness at 7-10°C (40-50°F) until early spring. Resume watering and provide good light.
PROPAGATION By seed or cuttings indoors in summer or autumn.
TRANSPLANTING TIME Spring.
FLOWERING TIME Spring through autumn. The flowers, which hang down, have a long calyx and a 4-petal corolla. Their colours range through white, purplish-red, purple and pink; the flowers are often bicoloured.
USES In flowerbeds, borders or shrubberies. The varieties with a prostrate habit are particularly suitable for growing in pots and hanging-baskets or as standards (tree form) in tubs.
CUTTING BACK Plants stored over winter can be cut back in autumn. New growth in spring can be pinched back for bushiness. Those varieties which have been treated as herbaceous perennials in milder climates can be cut back to ground level and the clumps mulched with leaves to protect them during the winter.
PESTS Aphids, red spider mites, whitefly.
DISEASES Grey mould.

Snowdrop
Galanthus nivalis

FAMILY *Amaryllidaceae.*
PLACE OF ORIGIN Europe.
TYPE OF PLANT Herbacous perennial, bulbous; free-growing; its light green leaves are long and narrow. There are several varieties, but they are rarely available from dealers.
HEIGHT 10-30 cm (4-12 ins), depending on the variety.
SOIL TYPE Average to rich, well drained soil.
MOISTURE Since they bloom in winter to early spring, often right through the snow, extra watering is not needed.
POSITION Sunny or shady but with plenty of light, especially in early spring.
CLIMATE Temperate.
PROPAGATION By seed from autumn to spring or by clump division. They will self-sow.
TRANSPLANTING TIME During or after flowering; the bulbs should be replanted in their new site immediately to avoid drying out. New bulbs are available from dealers in autumn.
FLOWERING TIME Often from January onwards even in the North. The white, pendulous flowers have small green markings on the inside tip of the petals. Seed-grown plants usually take five years to come into flower.
USES Naturalized in lawns or grouped in rock gardens and under trees.
PESTS Nematodes and the larvae of various insects that may damage the bulbs.
DISEASES Grey mould.

Gentian
Geniana acaulis (1)
Gentiana lutea (2)
Gentiana verna (3)

FAMILY *Gentianaceae*.
PLACE OF ORIGIN Europe.
TYPE OF PLANT Herbaceous perennial, free-growing; its leaves are glossy, oval and deciduous. *G. lutea* has an erect habit.
HEIGHT Up to 1-1.5 m (40-60 in) for *G. lutea*. 5-15 cm (2-6 ins) for *G. acaulis* and *G. verna*.
SOIL TYPE Limy for *G. verna* and *G. lutea* but acid for *G. acaulis*. *G. lutea* is a bog plant.
MOISTURE Watering should be well distributed to keep the ground cool and moist but without forming pockets of water.
POSITION Sunny to part shade for *G. lutea*, moderately sunny for *G. acaulis* and *G. verna*.
CLIMATE Temperate-cool; many gentians thrive on hills and mountains.
PROPAGATION By seed in autumn (*G. lutea*). By clump division in the spring (*G. verna, G. acaulis*).
TRANSPLANTING TIME Autumn and spring, but most gentians, once established, resent being disturbed.
FLOWERING TIME *G. verna* and *G. acaulis* have deep blue flowers in spring and *G. lutea* has yellow flowers in summer.
USES *G.verna* and *G. acaulis* are suitable for rock gardens and *G. lutea* for moist herbaceous borders or bog gardens or to stand alone.
DISEASES Root rot.

Ivy
Hedera helix

FAMILY *Araliaceae*.
PLACE OF ORIGIN Europe, western Asia, northern Africa.
TYPE OF PLANT Evergreen vine or creeper, hardy; dark green leathery leaves; some varieties have variegated leaves shaded from green to pale yellow and of different sizes. Many named varieties, varying in hardiness.
HEIGHT Up to 15-30 m (49-98 ft).
SOIL TYPE Moist, humus-rich.
MOISTURE The ground should be constantly rather damp.
POSITION Shade to part shade and not in direct sunlight.
CLIMATE Temperate-cold. Generally hardy to about −20°C (+4°F).
PROPAGATION By cuttings in summer or autumn.
TRANSPLANTING TIME Autumn or early spring.
FLOWERING TIME Summer, with small green-white flowers followed by black berries. Only adult plants flower and fruit.
USES As a cover for walls, stonework, etc. and as ground-cover in shade where grass will not grow. It also lends itself well to being grown in pots, both as a climbing and trailing plant indoors and in greenhouses.
CUTTING BACK Ivies that are climbing up walls should be shortened in early spring and any old branches removed. In other situations, the tip of each branch can be removed in the summer to make the plant branch out laterally and thus avoid long straggly growth.
PESTS Aphids, but red spider mites can be more serious indoors. Also scales.

Sunflower
Helianthus annuus

FAMILY *Compositae*.
PLACE OF ORIGIN North America.
TYPE OF PLANT Herbaceous, annual, with an erect habit and light green, heart shaped leaves.
HEIGHT 0.5-4 m (20 ins – 13 ft), according to the variety.
SOIL TYPE Any type of well drained soil.
MOISTURE Abundant watering.
POSITION Full sun.
CLIMATE Temperate.
PROPAGATION By seed in spring.
TRANSPLANTING TIME When the seedlings are 10 cm (4 ins) high, but the seedlings are not usually transplanted.
FLOWERING TIME Summer; each golden yellow head is very large and has a brown center. There are red-flowered varieties.
USES To provide patches of bright colour in a vegetable garden or to give height to a very wide and long herbaceous border. Cooking and salad oil is extracted from the seed kernels. The seeds are eaten by birds.
DISEASES Grey mould on the flowers.

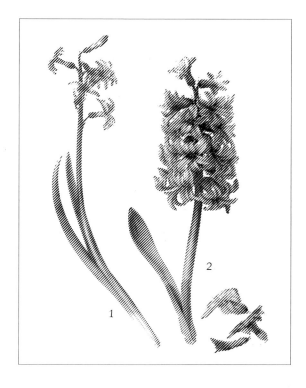

Hellebore or Christmas rose
Helleborus niger

FAMILY *Ranunculaceae.*
PLACE OF ORIGIN Central and southern Europe.
TYPE OF PLANT Herbaceous perennial, evergreen, rhizomatous. This plant is poisonous.
HEIGHT 30 cm (12 ins).
SOIL TYPE Limy, humus-rich, moist but well drained.
MOISTURE Regular watering as needed in summer.
POSITION Partial shade.
CLIMATE Temperate; this plant is very tolerant of the cold.
PROPAGATION By seed but germination is slow, requiring alternate freezing and thawing. By rhizome division in the spring.
TRANSPLANTING TIME Late summer but established plants resent being disturbed.
FLOWERING TIME The flowers are white, often tinged with pale pink and may appear from late autumn to early spring, depending on climate.
USES For borders, rock gardens and for naturalizing in woodlands. The flowers may be cut for arrangements.

Hibiscus
Hibiscus rosa-sinensis

FAMILY *Malvaceae.*
PLACE OF ORIGIN Asia.
TYPE OF PLANT Shrub, evergreen; its glossy dark green leaves are oval and tooth-edged.
HEIGHT 2-3 m (6½-10 ft) in really warm areas.
SOIL TYPE Light, organic, well drained.
MOISTURE Frequent watering, especially in hot spells.
POSITION Sunny.
CLIMATE Temperate-warm; in colder areas the hibiscus is grown in a large pot or tub and brought under cover during the winter to a plant room or greenhouse where it will get plenty of daylight.
PROPAGATION By cuttings in summer.
TRANSPLANTING TIME Late spring or autumn.
FLOWERING TIME Early summer to autumn; in its ideal tropical climate, the hibiscus will continue to bloom throughout the year. The flowers are quite large and its colours include dark red, orange, pink and yellow; some varieties are double and others semi-double.
USES For hedges and patches of colour in a garden; it is also well suited to being grown in pots on terraces, balconies.
CUTTING BACK The branches can be shortened in the spring.
PESTS Aphids, scale insects, red spider mites.

Hyacinth
Hyacinthus orientalis (1)
Hyacinthus romanus (2) (syn. *Bellevalia romana*)

FAMILY *Liliaceae.*
PLACE OF ORIGIN Eastern Europe, western Asia *(H. orientalis);* southern Europe *(H. romanus).*
TYPE OF PLANT Bulbous perennial, with long narrow, fleshy leaves.
HEIGHT 20-30 cm (8-12 ins), according to the variety.
SOIL TYPE Friable, well drained and fairly rich.
POSITION Sunny or semi-shaded.
CLIMATE Temperate. In cold areas the bulbs should be covered with a layer of leaves or straw over winter.
PROPAGATION By offsets from the bulbs, lifted after flowering and when leaves have died.
TRANSPLANTING TIME In the autumn for spring flowering and for forced winter flowering. Specially treated bulbs can give blooms at Christmas.
FLOWERING TIME Early spring. A winter flowering can be obtained earlier by using bulbs specially treated for forcing, as mentioned above. Regular forced bulbs should bloom indoors in 10 weeks or so. The colours of the *H. orientalis* varieties range through white, pink, yellow, red and several shades of blue. *H. romanus* has sweetly scented greenish-white flowers and several flowering stems.
USES For flowerbeds, pots and tubs; hyacinth bulbs can also be grown with water alone in hyacinth vases (available from bulb dealers), goblets and carafes.
DISEASES Bulb rot.

English Holly
Ilex aquifolium

FAMILY *Aquifoliacea.*
PLACE OF ORIGIN Europe, Mediterranean basin, the Caucasus.
TYPE OF PLANT Evergreen tree, often self-sown, with an erect habit and pyramidal head. Its glossy, dark green leaves have wavy, prickly edges. There are many varieties whose sizes, habits and foliage vary considerably. Sexes are on different plants, so male and female trees are needed for berries.
HEIGHT To 10 m (33 ft) or more, according to the variety and climate.
SOIL TYPE Any type of fertile, moist acid soil.
MOISTURE Regular watering – very frequent in hot weather.
POSITION Sunny, especially for the variegated-leafed varieties; all the others will grow in semi-shade although too much shade prevents flowers – and berries.
CLIMATE Temperate. Not hardy enough for cold dry Midwest.
PROPAGATION By seed and, in summer, by cuttings.
TRANSPLANTING TIME Autumn or spring.
FLOWERING TIME Spring. It has small, insignificant whitish flowers. If there are male plants near female plants, the flowers on the latter will mature into bright red, decorative berries.
USES As hedges and as single plants, which may either be left to follow their natural habit or trimmed into a shape.
CUTTING BACK This need only be done to control the shape. Such pruning can be done at Christmas and the greens used indoors. When grown as a hedge, trim in the spring.
PESTS Leaf miners, which attack the foliage of American holly, sometimes also infest English holly.

Iris
Iris pallida (1)
Iris pseudacorus (2)

FAMILY *Iridaceae.*
PLACE OF ORIGIN *I. pallida:* Austria, Italy, Yugoslavia; *I. pseudacorus:* Europe, northern Africa and widely naturalized in eastern North America.
TYPE OF PLANT Rhizomatous perennial, with long slender leaves which grow upwards.
HEIGHT 1-1.5 m (40-60 ins).
SOIL TYPE Any type for *I. pallida. I. pseudacorus* is suitable for a watery position at the edge of a pool or stream; it can be planted in water as deep as 45 cm (18 ins).
MOISTURE *I. pallida* does not usually require watering. *I. pseudacorus* needs a great deal of watering if grown on dry ground.
POSITION Sunny.
CLIMATE Temperate.
PROPAGATION By rhizome division after flowering and by seed.
TRANSPLANTING TIME Early summer *(I. pallida);* spring or autumn *(I. pseudacorus).*
FLOWERING TIME Spring to early summer. Colours range through light blue, purple, violet, white, according to the variety. in *I. pallida.* Early summer, with yellow flowers, sometimes striped, *in I. pseudacorus.*
USES For splashes of colour in borders, flowerbeds or in isolation; they grow well in large pots for a time on balconies, terraces, patios and are excellent as cut flowers *(I. pallida).* Naturalized at the edges of pools and small lakes, on the banks of streams *(I. pseudacorus).*
CUTTING BACK Dead flowers should be removed every day.
PESTS Aphids and iris borers.
DISEASES Rhizome rot and canker, viruses and grey mould.

Jasmine
Jasminum floribundum (1)
Jasminum nudiflorum (2)
Jasminum officinale (3)
Jasminum sambac (4)
Jasminum sp. (5)

FAMILY *Oleaceae.*
PLACE OF ORIGIN India, China.
TYPE OF PLANT Climbing, with long thin trailing shoots and deciduous leaves.
HEIGHT 1.5-15 m (5-50 ft), according to the species.
SOIL TYPE Any type of well drained soil.
MOISTURE Regular watering.
POSITION Sunny and sheltered for all the species; *J. nudiflorum* will even thrive in semi-shade.
CLIMATE Temperate-warm. Only *J. nudiflorum* is suitable for colder climates.
PROPAGATION Semi-hardwood cuttings can be taken in late summer. Layering can be started in autumn. Propagation can also be by seed.
TRANSPLANTING TIME Autumn or spring.
FLOWERING TIME Through the summer, according to the species, except for *J. nudiflorum* which blooms in the winter – early spring in the North. This latter species has golden-yellow flowers while the others have white and even pink flowers.
USES As climbers over fences, pergolas, trellises, rocks, banks. They also lend themselves well to being grown in pots on balconies and terraces, although they always need some kind of support over which they can clamber.
CUTTING BACK The branches can be thinned out in early spring. The branches that have flowered on *J. nudiflorum* should immediately be cut back to 8 cm (3½ ins) from the ground.
PESTS Aphids and scale insects.

Sweet bay
Laurus nobilis

FAMILY *Lauraceae.*
PLACE OF ORIGIN Mediterranean basin.
TYPE OF PLANT Shrub or small tree, evergreen, free-growing in the Mediterranean regions, with very aromatic, dark green, leathery leaves. Each plant is either male or female.
HEIGHT 2-7 m (6½-23 ft).
SOIL TYPE Any type.
POSITION Sunny.
CLIMATE Temperate. In a sheltered position, the sweet bay will endure some frost, but in the North must be wintered in a cool room or greenhouse.
PROPAGATION By cuttings of the side shoots at the end of the summer. Also by layering in late summer and by seed.
TRANSPLANTING TIME Spring.
FLOWERING TIME Spring. Both male and female flowers are small and pale yellow.
USES As isolated shrubs or as hedges. The sweet bay makes an excellent pot or tub plant and can even be trained as a standard (tree form). Its aromatic leaves are the "bay leaf" used in the kitchen.
PESTS Scale insects.
DISEASES Mildew, leaf spot.

Madonna lily
Lilium candidum

FAMILY *Liliaceae.*
PLACE OF ORIGIN Balkan Peninsula, Asia Minor.
TYPE OF PLANT Bulbous perennial, hardy, with an erect habit. It throws out roots from the stem as well as from the bulb.
HEIGHT 90 cm-120 cm (3-4 ft).
SOIL TYPE Well drained garden soil, slightly alkaline.
MOISTURE Moderate watering, which should be increased during period of growth.
POSITION Sunny and sheltered.
CLIMATE Temperate.
PROPAGATION By separating established bulbs in late summer or by detaching the bulb scales and/or aerial bulbils at the same time and planting them shallowly in prepared trays or flats.
TRANSPLANTING TIME Late summer to autumn for new bulbs from dealers and for bulbs obtained from division. Plant them so their tops are only 5 cm (2 in) below the surface.
FLOWERING TIME Early summer. The white flowers are heavily scented and shaped like a chalice.
USES To give height in borders and as cut flowers.
PESTS Aphids and lily beetle.
DISEASES Root rot, grey mould.

Tulip tree
Liriodendron tulipifera

FAMILY *Magnoliaceae.*
PLACE OF ORIGIN Massachusetts to Florida and Mississippi.
TYPE OF PLANT A majestic flowering tree with deciduous leaves, which turn pale yellow in the autumn.
HEIGHT To 60 m (200 ft), with a broad head.
SOIL TYPE Lime-free, humus-rich.
MOISTURE It prefers moist soil.
POSITION Sunny or semi-shaded.
CLIMATE Temperate.
PROPAGATION By seed sown outdoors when ripe for germination the next spring. Self-sows freely.
TRANSPLANTING TIME Transplanting is difficult and should only be done in early spring. Seedlings and young trees can be moved readily though, again spring being the preferred time.
FLOWERING TIME Early summer. The large, tulip-shaped flowers are pale green and orange-yellow.
USES As highly decorative trees in parklands and on large properties.

Magnolia
Magnolia grandiflora (1)
Magnolia liliflora (2) (syn. *M. quinquepeta*)

FAMILY *Magnoliaceae*.
PLACE OF ORIGIN China for *M. liliflora*; N. Carolina to Florida and Texas for *M. grandiflora*.
TYPE OF PLANT *M. grandiflora:* a tree with an erect habit, compact and slightly conical; its evergreen, leathery leaves are dark green and glossy. *M. liliflora:* a shrub with light green, deciduous foliage.
HEIGHT About 20-25 m (65½-82 ft) for *M. grandiflora;* 4-5 m (13-16½ ft) for *M. liliflora*.
SOIL TYPE Acid or neutral, deep, humus-rich and moist.
MOISTURE Water should not be allowed to stand over the roots.
POSITION Full sun or semi-shade.
CLIMATE Temperate-mild. Although both species will survive on the East Coast beyond Washington D.C., neither is reliably hardy in the North.
PROPAGATION By cuttings or layering in spring-summer.
TRANSPLANTING TIME Autumn or late winter, after 2-3 years.
FLOWERING TIME *M. liliflora:* purplish-red flowers in the spring. *M. grandiflora:* very showy white flowers in late spring to early summer.
USES In gardens and parklands as splashes of colour or isolated specimens.
CUTTING BACK The head of *M. liliflora* can be pruned back into shape after flowering.
DISEASES Grey mould, leaf spot, mildew.

Chamomile
Matricaria chamomilla (1) (syn. *Tripleurospermum maritimum*)
Anthemis nobilis (2) (syn. *Chamaemelum nobile*)

FAMILY *Compositae*.
PLACE OF ORIGIN Europe, Asia *(M. chamomilla);* south-west Europe *(A. nobilis)*.
TYPE OF PLANT *M. chamomilla:* herbaceous or short-lived perennial, free-growing, with a branched, erect stem and feathery leaves; it is strongly aromatic. *A. nobilis:* herbaceous perennial, forming green cushions, also aromatic.
HEIGHT 30-60 cm (12-24 ins) for *M. chamomilla*. 15-25 cm (6-10 ins) for *A. nobilis*.
SOIL TYPE Both are suited to a variety of soil types, including rather dry ones.
MOISTURE No special requirements.
POSITION Sunny.
PROPAGATION By seed in the spring or autumn or by clump division in spring or autumn. Both plants self-sow and are naturalized in North America.
TRANSPLANTING TIME Spring.
FLOWERING TIME Late spring to summer; the flower heads are typical daisies.
USES As medicinal plants with calming and digestive properties. *A. nobilis* makes a charming flowering carpet but cannot take much foot traffic; there is a non-flowering variety, which is more suitable as a lawn. It is often listed as *Anthemis nobilis* "Treneague" in catalogs.
CUTTING BACK *A. nobilis* should be cut back to the base in the spring to encourage the growth of the side shoots.

Forget-me-not
Myosotis alpestris

FAMILY *Boraginaceae*.
PLACE OF ORIGIN Europe.
TYPE OF PLANT Perennial, usually grown as a hardy biennial; its light green leaves are deciduous and oblong.
HEIGHT 10-15 cm (4-6 ins).
SOIL TYPE Any type, preferably rich in organic materials and moist.
MOISTURE Regular and frequent watering.
POSITION Semi-shade.
CLIMATE Temperate-cool.
PROPAGATION By seed in late spring to early summer to achieve flowering plants the following spring. Tends to self-sow.
TRANSPLANTING TIME Autumn.
FLOWERING TIME Spring. The flowers are small and light blue; there are also white, pink and carmine-red varieties.
USES For borders, rock gardens and as cut flowers.
DISEASES Grey mould.

Myrtle
Myrtus communis

FAMILY *Myrtaceae.*
PLACE OF ORIGIN Mediterranean basin, Asia.
TYPE OF PLANT An evergreen shrub with a
compact shape; its dark green, oval leaves are
glossy and aromatic; there are also varieties with
smaller or variegated leaves.
HEIGHT 50 cm-1.5 m (20-60 ins)
SOIL TYPE Well drained.
MOISTURE Water during dry summer weather.
POSITION Sunny and sheltered.
CLIMATE In a mild region, the myrtle thrives
out-of-doors, in fact it grows wild in the
scrublands of the Mediterranean coast; in colder
areas, it has to be grown indoors in a sunny
window or in a greenhouse.
PROPAGATION By cuttings of non-flowering
shoots in early summer.
TRANSPLANTING TIME Late spring.
FLOWERING TIME Summer; its small white
flowers are sweetly scented.
USES For shrubberies and hedges; as an
aromatic herb in cooking.
CUTTING BACK The plant can be trimmed back
into shape after flowering; hedges should be
pruned in the spring and summer to keep them
neat.

Narcissus
Narcissus poeticus (1)
Narcissus sp. (2)
Narcissus x *hortorum* (3)

FAMILY *Amaryllidaceae.*
PLACE OF ORIGIN Europe, Mediterranean basin,
Asia.
TYPE OF PLANT Bulbous perennial, with light
green lance head shaped leaves.
HEIGHT 8-50 cm (3-20 ins), according to the
variety.
SOIL TYPE Open, fertile, well drained, moist.
MOISTURE Regular watering after planting new
bulbs in autumn. Spring rainfall adequate in
most regions.
POSITION Sunny or semi-shaded.
CLIMATE Temperate-cool. Narcissus or daffodils
are very hardy except for a few kinds, such as the
paperwhite narcissus.
PROPAGATION By separating the bulb's offsets
when the leaves have yellowed, or in autumn.
TRANSPLANTING TIME Autumn.
FLOWERING TIME Early to late spring, according
to the varieties and climate. The flowers are
white or yellow and sometimes bicoloured, with
a short or long orange corona (trumpet or
center). *N. poeticus* has a small, scented flower
with a short yellow corona.
USES For borders, flowerbeds, in front of shrubs,
under high-branched trees and in lawns and
fields; they grow well in pots and the bulbs can
be forced for flowering indoors during the
winter. Certain kinds (paperwhite narcissus)
can be grown indoors in pebbles and water.
CUTTING BACK The leaves should not be
removed until they have turned brown and the
plants become dormant.
PESTS Lesser bulb fly may attack bulbs.
DISEASES Grey mould, basal bulb rot.

Lotus
Nelumbo nucifera
(syn. *Nelumbium speciosum*)

FAMILY *Nymphaeaceae.*
PLACE OF ORIGIN Tropical and sub-tropical
Asia.
TYPE OF PLANT Aquatic perennial, rhizomatous;
its leaves, which are held above the water rather
than floating on it, can be as large as 80 cm (32
ins) in diameter. It has become naturalized in
several Italian lakes.
HEIGHT 50-100 cm (20-40 ins) above the level of
the water.
SOIL TYPE It must be enriched with good manure
and not be less than 30 cm (12 ins) deep. The
depth of the water can vary from 0.5-2 m (20-80
ins).
POSITION Sunny or semi-shade in hot areas.
CLIMATE Temperate. In places where the winters
are very cold, the rhizomes can be taken out of
the water in the autumn and stored at 10°C (50°F)
in damp sand until the spring. In deep water, the
tubers often survive in the North.
PROPAGATION By seed or by dividing the
rhizomes so that there is at least one shoot on
each piece.
TRANSPLANTING TIME In the spring. As soon as
the rhizomes have been separated, they should
be planted immediately.
FLOWERING TIME Summer. The buds are
egg-shaped and the fragrant flowers large and
either pink or shading into red. The size varies
according to the variety, of which there are
several.

Oleander
Nerium oleander

FAMILY *Apocynaceae*.
PLACE OF ORIGIN Mediterranean basin.
TYPE OF PLANT Shrub or small tree, evergreen with lance-head shaped leaves, which curve slightly downwards; it grows wild in its natural environment. It is a poisonous plant.
HEIGHT Up to 4-6 cm (13-20 ft).
SOIL TYPE Any type.
MOISTURE Abundant and frequent watering, especially in the summer.
POSITION Sunny or semi-shade.
CLIMATE Temperate-hot. In the North, tub-grown plants are wintered in greenhouses and brought outdoors in summer.
PROPAGATION By seed in April. By cuttings in summer. They will root in water.
TRANSPLANTING TIME Spring or autumn.
FLOWERING TIME Early summer to autumn. The single or double flowers are grouped in clusters; the colours vary considerably, the most usual being pink and the next red and white.
USES As hedges or in large pots or tubs on porches, terraces, patios.
CUTTING BACK Branches that have flowered can be shortened in the autumn and weak growth cut out altogether; if the plants are being grown as small trees, the heads should be trimmed into shape and any shoots removed from the trunks.
PESTS Scale insects and mealybugs.
DISEASES Scabs or tumours caused by a fungus and leaf spot.

Waterlily
Nymphaea alba

FAMILY *Nymphaeaceae*.
PLACE OF ORIGIN Europe, Asia.
TYPE OF PLANT Aquatic, rhizomatous perennial, very long-lived, hardy; its leathery, heart-shaped leaves float on the surface of ponds and lakes where other waterlilies normally live.
HEIGHT 0.5-3 m (20 ins-10 ft).
SOIL TYPE It must have a depth of 20-30 cm (8-12 ins). The best soil is one of clay that is free from peat moss or leafmould, but contains some decayed manure. To keep the water clean and clear to a depth of at least 50 cm (20 ins), add a thin layer of pea gravel or sand. The plants are often grown in baskets or pots set on the bottom of the pool.
POSITION Sunny.
CLIMATE Temperate. This waterlily species is hardy in the North, but many others are not.
PROPAGATION By division of the rhizomes in spring. Also by seed enclosed in clay and dropped in the pond.
TRANSPLANTING TIME Spring.
FLOWERING TIME The whole summer. The flowers are shaped rather like goblets, with long, pointed white petals and yellow stamens.
USES As decorative plants in garden pools, fountain basins, ponds. They can also be grown in watertight containers, with a depth of 60 cm (24 ins), on terraces and patios.
CUTTING BACK Every third spring, the weak parts of the rhizomes should be removed and the roots shortened.
PESTS Aphids and larvae of various insects in the roots.
DISEASES Leaf rot.

Hardy (Terrestrial) Orchids
Cypripedium calceolus (1)
Ophrys sp. (2)

FAMILY *Orchidaceae*.
PLACE OF ORIGIN *C. calceolus*: Europe, Asia and yellow varieties *parviflorum* and *pubescens* in North America. *Ophrys sp.*: Europe, British Isles and western Asia.
TYPE OF PLANT Herbaceous perennial, with an erect stem, evergreen or deciduous, its long leaves rather leathery. *C. calceolus* is sometimes called Venus's slipper, yellow lady's-slipper, and small yellow moccasin flower.
HEIGHT 25-60 cm (10-24 ins).
SOIL TYPE Well drained, acid and enriched with leafmould and/or peat moss for *C. calceolus*. *Ophrys* species prefer some lime added to their soil.
MOISTURE Regular watering during summer droughts.
POSITION Generally part shady.
CLIMATE Temperate-cool. As these are mostly indigenous to cold climates, they prefer regions with short, cool summers.
PROPAGATION By clump division after flowering, although in general, the less root disturbance the better.
TRANSPLANTING TIME After flowering.
FLOWERING TIME End of spring *(C. calceolus)*; spring-early summer *(Ophrys sp.)* The flowers have chestnut-brown sepals and a pale yellow enlarged lower lip (labellum), reminiscent of a slipper *(C. calceolus)*. The greenish-yellow sepals and labellum of the *Ophrys sp.* look rather like an insect.
USES Wild flower and rock gardens.
PESTS Aphids, scale insects, red spiders, rodents which eat the tubers.
DISEASES Rotting of the whole plant, rust, leaf spot.

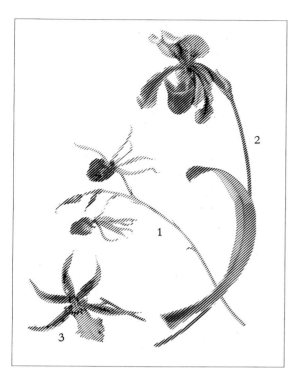

Tropical Orchids
Epidendrum cochleatum (1)
Paphiopedilum sp. (2)
Brassia sp. (3)

FAMILY *Orchidaceae.*
PLACE OF ORIGIN Tropical Asiatic regions
(Paphiopedilum sp.) and similar areas of North
and South America *(E. cochleatum, Brassia sp.).*
TYPE OF PLANT Herbaceous perennial, growing
in clumps, with ribbon-like leaves
(Paphiopedilum sp.). Heart shaped leaves,
pseudo bulbs *(E. cochleatum, Brassia sp.).*
Mostly epiphytes and under cultivation, grown
as pot plants.
HEIGHT Up to 30 cm (12 ins).
SOIL TYPE Dried osmunda fiber and sphagnum
moss or fir tree bark and moss, often mixed with
perlite.
MOISTURE A moist atmosphere is essential; if
necessary, the leaves should be sprayed
frequently with lime-free water.
POSITION Generally well lighted including
sunshine in winter, but part shade in summer.
CLIMATE For greenhouses, very damp and warm
but ventilated in summer; minimum winter
temperature between 5-16°C (41-61°F), at night,
warmer in daytime according to the species.
PROPAGATION By clump division in the spring
or after flowering.
TRANSPLANTING TIME After flowering.
FLOWERING TIME Winter to early summer,
according to variety. The flowers are single and
range in colour through brown, green and
yellow with marks or veining *(Paphiopedilum
sp.* and *Brassia sp.).* The shell shaped flowers of
E. cochleatum, borne on spikes, are yellow and a
purplish-blue.
USES As ornamental plants, mostly for
collectors, and cut flowers, usually in corsages.
PESTS Aphids, scale insects, red spider mites.
DISEASES Leaf spot, rust, rotting of the whole
plant.

Tropical Orchids
Cymbidium hybrids (1)
Dendrobium phalaenopsis (2)
Epidendrum ibaguense (3) (syn. *E. radicans*)
Phalaenopsis sp. (4)

FAMILY *Orchidaceae.*
PLACE OF ORIGIN Central and South America *(E.
ibaguense);* tropical Asia and Australia
(Cymbidium species – hybrids from specialists
world-wide); India, Indonesia, Australia
(Phalaenopsis sp.); Australia to New Guinea *(D.
phalaenopsis).*
TYPE OF PLANT Herbaceous perennial, with
long narrow evergreen leaves. They also have
pseudo bulbs with the exception of the
Phalaenopsis, which has a short stem with fleshy
leaves and very long aerial roots.
HEIGHT Up to 1.22 m (4 ft) or more.
SOIL TYPE Dried osmunda fern fiber and
sphagnum moss or fir-tree bark and moss; for the
Cymbidium one part of garden soil can be
added, as most are terrestrial.
MOISTURE A moist atmosphere such as in a
greenhouse is essential; frequent spraying of the
leaves with tepid, lime-free water is helpful.
POSITION Semi-shady until autumn, then sun.
CLIMATE A humid and warm but ventilated
greenhouse, with a minimum night time
temperature of 10-15°C (50-59°F) in the winter.
PROPAGATION By clump division in the spring
or after flowering.
TRANSPLANTING TIME After flowering.
FLOWERING TIME Autumn, winter, spring,
according to the species. The flowers, usually
borne on long stalks, are in all colours except
blue.
USES As ornamental plants especially prized by
collectors and as cut flowers for corsages,
mostly grown by professionals.
PESTS Aphids, scale insects, red spider mites.
DISEASES Rotting of the whole plant, often due to
overwatering, and various leaf spot diseases.

Corn Poppy
Papaver rhoeas

FAMILY *Papaveraceae.*
PLACE OF ORIGIN Europe, Asia.
TYPE OF PLANT Herbaceous annual; its light
green, hairy leaves are deeply cut into tapering
lobes.
HEIGHT 50-90 cm (20-36 ins).
SOIL TYPE Any type of well drained, fairly dry,
soil.
MOISTURE Regular watering, as necessary.
POSITION Sunny.
CLIMATE Temperate.
PROPAGATION By seed in early autumn or very
early spring.
FLOWERING TIME Summer. The red flowers are
borne on long stems; usually single, a few
varieties are double. Colours include white,
pink, pale yellow and apricot.
USES In borders and flowerbeds.

Passion flower
Passiflora caerulea

FAMILY *Passifloraceae.*
PLACE OF ORIGIN Brazil to Argentina.
TYPE OF PLANT Climbing, evergreen, vigorous, fairly hardy, with lobed leaves spreading out like the fingers of a hand.
HEIGHT Up to 6 m (24 ft).
SOIL TYPE Well drained garden soil, better if slightly acid.
MOISTURE Abundant watering from spring to autumn, especially for plants growing in small pots.
POSITION Sunny and sheltered.
CLIMATE Preferably mild, although it grows well in many parts of the Mediterranean countries. Frost will damage its top growth but new growth will invariably spring up from the base.
However, it will not survive prolonged freezing temperatures, and must be grown indoors in the North.
PROPAGATION By cuttings in the spring and by seed.
TRANSPLANTING TIME Spring.
FLOWERING TIME Summer to autumn. The flowers are quite large and flat, in colours that vary from white to light blue and red; the edible egg-shaped fruit is orange.
USES To cover walls, pergolas, fences and trellis-work. It also grows well in pots but always needs something to which it can cling, such as stiff netting, taut string, trellis.
CUTTING BACK In the spring any branches damaged by frost should be removed as well as those that are growing awkwardly on the supports. Secondary branches can be cut back to 15 cm (6 ins).
PESTS Nematodes.
DISEASES Cucumber mosaic virus may attack the leaves in the winter or spring.

Geranium or Pelargonium
Pelargonium × hortorum

FAMILY *Geraniaceae.*
PLACE OF ORIGIN South Africa.
TYPE OF PLANT Semi-shrublike perennial, evergreen or deciduous. The leaves may be lobed.
HEIGHT 60-100 cm (24-40 ins).
SOIL TYPE Fertile, well drained.
MOISTURE Abundant watering during growth and then decreased; the soil should only be kept slightly damp during the winter resting period by giving very small amounts of water or none at all, depending on the moisture present.
POSITION Sunny or very light shade.
CLIMATE If the weather is mild throughout the winter, the plants can remain out-of-doors. In colder areas they should be brought indoors to a sunny window in a cool but frost-free room. Some varieties, which originate from colder countries, cannot tolerate hot summer weather.
PROPAGATION By cuttings in spring or late summer. By seed (indoors in the North) in winter with a minimum temperature of 18°C (65°F).
TRANSPLANTING TIME Spring.
FLOWERING TIME Spring-autumn, and into winter if conditions are favourable. Colours of the flowers range from white to mauvish-blue, pink, scarlet, dark red and mauve, variegated.
USES In flowerbeds and borders. They are particularly suitable as pot plants for balconies, window-boxes and other containers.
CUTTING BACK The adult plants should be cut back to one-third of their height in late summer if the plants are to be brought indoors.
PESTS Mealybugs, white flies and aphids.
DISEASES Various virus diseases and some bacterial rots.

Petunia
Petunia × hybrida

FAMILY *Solanaceae.*
PLACE OF ORIGIN Petunia species are native to Brazil and southwestern South America.
TYPE OF PLANT Tender herbaceous perennial (but grown as an annual) with slightly hairy, oval leaves. The many hybrids listed in seed catalogs are divided into four classes, according to form or habit: "multiflora," "grandiflora," "nana compacta" (dwarf or bedding), "pendula" (long and trailing).
HEIGHT 20-60 cm (8-24 ins).
SOIL TYPE Light and well drained.
MOISTURE Abundant watering.
POSITION Very sunny.
CLIMATE When grown as an annual, it is suitable for various climates, but may sulk in hot, humid weather.
PROPAGATION By seed indoors in the North in early spring or later in a seedbed; in mild climates, seed can be scattered over its flowering site. Plants freely self-sow, but the progeny may not resemble their highly hybridized parents.
TRANSPLANTING TIME Spring.
FLOWERING TIME Spring to autumn, depending on climate. The bell-like flowers cover a wide range of colours, including white, pink, red, violet, lavender and yellow; these may be in single colours or two colours in boldly contrasting stripes and the flowers may be single or double, according to the variety. Most are very fragrant.
USES In borders and flowerbeds. The petunia is very suitable for growing in pots, tubs, including hanging containers.

Potentilla
Potentilla fruticosa (1)
Potentilla reptans (2)

FAMILY *Rosaceae*.
PLACE OF ORIGIN Europe.
TYPE OF PLANT Hardy shrub with a compact habit and light green leaves shaped like small hands arranged on opposite sides of the stem (*P. fruticosa*); herbaceous, hardy, perennial with creeping habitat, and adventitious roots and lobed leaves with small teeth on the margins (*P. reptans*). The latter is commonly known as cinquefoil and *P. fruticosa*, as bush cinquefoil.
HEIGHT 5 cm (2 ins) (*P. reptans*); about 91-120 cm (36-48 ins) (*P. fruticosa*).
SOIL TYPE Light, moist, well drained to more average dry soil.
MOISTURE *P. reptans* should be watered in dry weather.
POSITION Sunny.
CLIMATE Temperate.
PROPAGATION By stolons (*P. reptans*). By clump divisions, and cuttings of named varieties or seed in the spring (*P. fruticosa*).
TRANSPLANTING TIME Spring or autumn.
FLOWERING TIME Golden-yellow flowers in the summer; some varieties, with white or orange flowers, continue flowering into autumn.
USES In borders and in pots. *P. reptans* makes an excellent ground-cover and can also be used in rock gardens.

English Primrose
Primula vulgaris

FAMILY *Primulaceae*.
PLACE OF ORIGIN Southern Europe. Widely naturalized in British Isles.
TYPE OF PLANT Hardy herbaceous perennial, with light green, deciduous, oval leaves with crinkled edges; it grows in compact clumps.
HEIGHT 10-15 cm (4-6 ins).
SOIL TYPE Light, rich in organic matter and acid to slightly acid.
MOISTURE Frequent watering, especially in the summer.
POSITION Semi-shady. In full shade, there will be few flowers.
CLIMATE Cool and moist, such as in the British Isles and in the Pacific Northwest and along the Atlantic Coast.
PROPAGATION By seed in spring or autumn. By division of old clumps after flowering.
TRANSPLANTING TIME End of the winter after flowering or late summer.
FLOWERING TIME Spring. The flowers are borne in clusters or singly and are butter-yellow in colour. Cultivated hybrids are also available in white, purple, red, pink and orange.
USES In borders and rock gardens, as ground-cover in shrubberies, along woodland paths, on grassy banks and naturalized in grass under trees or near brooks and ponds. They also grow well in pots.
PESTS Slugs and snails, which eat the leaves and flowers, as well as larvae of various insects that may chew the roots.
DISEASES Root rot, grey mould and rust.

Flowering Cherry
Prunus avium

FAMILY *Rosaceae*.
PLACE OF ORIGIN Central Europe, eastern Asia.
TYPE OF PLANT Vigorous, deciduous tree with an erect habit and a truncated conical head; its green, slightly glossy leaves turn crimson-bronze in the autumn. *P. avium* (sweet cherry) and *P. cerasus* (sour cherry) are the parents of the now widely grown fruit trees that produce dessert and pie cherries. The Japanese flowering cherry is *P. serralata* and a handsome ornamental in spring.
HEIGHT Up to 20 m (65 ft).
SOIL TYPE Well drained, moist garden soil.
MOISTURE Regular watering but without forming pockets of water.
POSITION Sunny.
CLIMATE Cool in most northern regions but sensitive to air pollution.
PROPAGATION By seed or, for named varieties, cuttings and grafting.
TRANSPLANTING TIME Spring or autumn.
FLOWERING TIME Spring. The flowers are white and single; there are named double varieties of both species.
USES In orchards or as specimens; however, sweet cherries require other cherry trees nearby as pollinizers if fruits are desired.
CUTTING BACK It is advisable to prune these trees as little as possible as they do not heal easily.
PESTS Aphids, tent caterpillars, maggots and larvae of the cherry sawfly.
DISEASES Leaf curl, mildew, and leaf spot.

Flowering Peach
Prunus persica

FAMILY *Rosaceae.*
PLACE OF ORIGIN China.
TYPE OF PLANT Small tree with deciduous, lance head shaped leaves and a round head.
HEIGHT Up to 5-7 m (16½-23 ft).
SOIL TYPE Friable and well drained, preferably acid.
MOISTURE Regular watering, abundant during dry periods.
POSITION Sunny.
CLIMATE Temperate-cool; it does not like spring frosts that may kill the flower buds.
PROPAGATION By seed and by grafting.
TRANSPLANTING TIME In autumn or at the end of the winter in northern regions.
FLOWERING TIME Early spring. The flowers of the typical species are pink and bear fruit. There are also some purely ornamental varieties with double and semi-double flowers in white, deep pink and red.
USES *P. persica* is grown as a fruit-tree. The ornamental varieties are grown both in gardens and in large pots on terraces, patios and roof gardens.
CUTTING BACK The fruiting trees can be pruned at the end of the winter. The ornamental peach trees are partly pruned when the branches are gathered in the spring for indoor decoration and the task can be completed as soon as the flowers have faded.
PESTS Aphids, scale insects, red spider mites, larvae of the oriental fruit moth and peach tree borers. Bacterial leaf spot and peach leaf curl.

Pomegranate
Punica granatum

FAMILY *Punicaceae.*
PLACE OF ORIGIN Southeast Asia; naturalized in the Mediterranean basin.
TYPE OF PLANT Small, deciduous tree with a bushy habit. It is quite spiny and has small, glossy, leathery leaves.
HEIGHT Up to 4-6 m (13-20 ft); there are also dwarf varieties of 30-60 cm (12-24 ins) high.
SOIL TYPE Moist and fertile.
MOISTURE Requires watering during hot weather.
POSITION Sunny.
CLIMATE Mild. Grown in Florida and on the West Coast and although it tolerates winter frosts quite well, it must be grown in pots indoors in the North.
PROPAGATION By seed in spring or by cuttings or layering .
FLOWERING TIME Spring-early summer. The flowers are scarlet-red and the fruit, which is edible, ripens in autumn.
USES As a little ornamental tree and for its fruit. The dwarf varieties are particularly suited to being grown in pots and may be trained as bonsai.
CUTTING BACK Trimmed into shape as needed at the end of the winter.

Alpenrose Rhododendron
Rhododendron ferrugineum

FAMILY *Ericaceae.*
PLACE OF ORIGIN Mountains of central Europe.
TYPE OF PLANT Hardy shrub with evergreen, scaly leaves, often rather twiggy with an erect habit and rounded head; the leaves are oval or lance head shaped.
HEIGHT 90-120 cm (3-4 ft).
SOIL TYPE Acid, open and well drained. Mix peat moss in soil.
MOISTURE Frequent and regular watering during drought.
POSITION Semi-shady, light and sheltered.
CLIMATE Temperate-cool.
PROPAGATION By seed indoors in autumn-spring; by layering started in spring.
TRANSPLANTING TIME Spring or autumn.
FLOWERING TIME Spring. The funnel-shaped flowers are small and rose-red in colour.
USES This is a good rhododendron for sunny rock gardens, which duplicate its mountainous origin.
CUTTING BACK Trim into shape after flowering. Rhododendrons do not need much pruning.

Old Roses
Rosa canina (1)
Rosa gallica (2)
Rosa pendulina (3)
Rosa rugosa (4)

FAMILY *Rosaceae.*
PLACE OF ORIGIN Southern Europe, western Asia *(R. gallica);* Europe, *(R. pendulina);* Europe, Western Asia *(R. canina);* Asia *(R. rugosa).* The genus *Rosa* includes over 100 species with numerous varieties and hybrids divided into several groups or classes.
TYPE OF PLANT Deciduous shrubs, thorny, with a bushy, well-branched habit and compound leaves with an irregular number of leaflets arranged in pairs on opposite sides of the leaf stem and with a terminal leaflet.
HEIGHT 2-5 m (6½-16½ ft).
SOIL TYPE Average to good garden soil, well drained, preferably slightly acid.
MOISTURE Abundant watering during the flowering period.
POSITION Sunny.
CLIMATE Temperate; they can tolerate the cold winters of most northern regions. *R. rugosa* is especially winter-hardy.
PROPAGATION By seed sown outdoors in autumn for spring germination, cuttings and grafting in summer.
TRANSPLANTING TIME Spring or autumn.
FLOWERING TIME Spring to early summer and scattered blooms to the end of summer for *R. rugosa.* The flowers, although single, are quite showy and have a delicate perfume; they are white, pale pink or dark red.
USES As hardy hedges and decorative shrubs.
CUTTING BACK In the spring, remove any branches damaged during the winter. However, the shrub roses usually need less pruning than hybrid tea roses.
PESTS Aphids.
DISEASES Mildew and black spot on foliage.

Hybrid Roses
Rosa hybrids

FAMILY *Rosaceae.*
PLACE OF ORIGIN They are derived from various species, most of which are native to Asia. Miniature roses are derived from *Rosa chinensis,* native to China, and hybrid tea roses.
TYPE OF PLANT Deciduous shrubs, fairly thorny; they can be branched, bushy, with a sarmentose or prostrate habit.
HEIGHT 20-30 cm up to 5-6 m (8-12 ins up to 16½-20 ft), according to the variety and type.
SOIL TYPE Garden soil, well drained and enriched with well rotted animal manure (if available) or organic materials.
MOISTURE Regular watering during the flowering period and droughts.
POSITION Sunny and sheltered from wind.
CLIMATE Temperate-cold.
PROPAGATION By cuttings or grafting in summer.
TRANSPLANTING TIME Spring and autumn in mild-winter regions.
FLOWERING TIME Late spring to summer and up to the end of summer for the varieties that have a second flowering. The flowers are showy and often sweetly scented; of different sizes, some are single and some double. Their colours include white, pink, yellow, orange, red and scarlet, in all their shades.
CUTTING BACK Pruning is carried out in spring.
USES Floribunda and grandiflora varieties can be grown as fairly low flowering hedges and in all-rose beds, usually combined with hybrid tea roses. Use climbers over arches, fences, pergolas or lattice work. Miniature roses are suitable as edgings for rose gardens but are best in pots and containers because of their low height. All types are suitable as cut flowers.
PESTS Aphids, scale insects, red spider mites, rose slugs and chafers and Japanese beetles.
DISEASES Grey mould, mildew and black spot.

Hybrid Tea Roses
Rosa hybrids

FAMILY *Rosaceae.*
PLACE OF ORIGIN Hybrid tea roses are mainly descended from crosses between the tender tea rose *(Rosa odorata)* of China and hybrid perpetual roses, themselves hybrids from crosses of various old roses and the tea rose. Hybrid tea roses have existed for over 50 years and their named varieties have been introduced from hybridizers all over the world, including New Zealand, Germany, France and the USA.
TYPE OF PLANT Deciduous shrubs, thorny, with a bushy habit, compound leaves with an irregular number of glossy or opaque leaflets arranged in pairs on opposite sides of the leaf stem and with a terminal leaflet.
HEIGHT 50-150 cm (20-60 ins).
SOIL TYPE Well drained garden soil but rich with well rotted manure and organic matters.
MOISTURE Regular watering, especially during the flowering period. Exceptionally heavy rain can damage the large-flowered varieties.
POSITION Sunny but sheltered from the wind in regions prone to this problem.
CLIMATE Temperate-cold. In very cold regions, bushes require winter protection.
PROPAGATION By cuttings or grafting in late summer.
TRANSPLANTING TIME Spring or autumn in mild-winter regions.
FLOWERING TIME Early summer to autumn. The flowers are showy; colours range through white or yellow, salmon pink, pink, crimson and lavender, depending on the variety.
USES In formal or informal all-rose gardens, as borders and, of course, as cut flowers.
CUTTING BACK Old wood should be cut out altogether in the spring and all other branches shortened.
PESTS Aphids, scale insects, red spider mites, rose chafers, Japanese beetles and rose slugs.
DISEASES Grey mould, mildew and black spot.

African violet
Saintpaulia ionantha

FAMILY *Gesneriaceae.*
PLACE OF ORIGIN Coastal Tanzania.
TYPE PLANT Tender herbaceous perennial, evergreen; its leaves are heart-shaped, fleshy and velvety.
HEIGHT 10 cm (4 ins), more or less, according to variety.
SOIL TYPE Lime-free humus-rich garden soil, which should be friable and permeable, or a soilless mix, packaged for house plants.
MOISTURE The growing medium should be kept moist but not soggy, with the pot standing on gravel on a water-filled tray to create all-round humidity. The leaves will rot if they become wet, or spot if watered with cold water in bright sunshine.
POSITION A bright position or in diffused sunlight or grow under fluorescent lights.
CLIMATE Very mild, with the winter temperature not falling below 14°C (57°F) at night and warmer during daylight.
PROPAGATION By leaf cuttings anytime and division of plants in summer also seed in the spring.
TRANSPLANTING TIME Usually late spring when flowering wanes; repot every two years or when plants become crowded.
FLOWERING TIME Most of the year, but plants tend to rest in summer. The single or double flowers are clustered on the stems that rise above the foliage. The colour range is pink, white, rose, mauve-blue and purple, according to the variety.
USES As a house plant.
PESTS Aphids, mealybugs and various mites.
DISEASES Rotting of cuttings and young plants. Avoid overwatering and do not stand the pots in water but above it on pebbles.

Rowan or Mountain Ash
Sorbus aucuparia

FAMILY *Rosaceae.*
PLACE OF ORIGIN Europe, Asia Minor.
TYPE OF PLANT Hardy tree or large shrub, deciduous, free-growing. The slender trunk is topped by an ovoid head; its leaves are compound with an irregular number of leaflets arranged in pairs on opposite sides of the leaf stem and with a terminal leaflet.
HEIGHT 10-12 m (33-40 ft); in exceptional cases, it reaches as high as 20 m (66 ft).
SOIL TYPE Any type of well drained, moist soil.
POSITION Sunny or semi-shaded.
CLIMATE Tolerates the cold well and thrives up to an altitude of 2,200 m (7,242 ft).
PROPAGATION By seed in autumn. Also root and stem cuttings.
TRANSPLANTING TIME Spring or autumn.
FLOWERING TIME May-July. The small, whitish flowers are borne in flat clusters. The berries are very showy, ripening to a bright reddish-orange in late summer to autumn and remaining into the winter.
USES As an ornamental tree, to prevent erosion in mountainous terrain, to line and give shade on roads and sidewalks as well as marking the boundaries of fields.

Broom
Spartium junceum (1) (syn. *Genista juncea)*
Genista tinctoria (2)

FAMILY *Leguminosae*
PLACE OF ORIGIN Mediterranean basin, Europe, northern Asia.
TYPE OF PLANT Shrubby habits, almost leafless, deciduous, sometimes spiny; they look like an evergreen because of the rich green of the young branches.
HEIGHT *Genista tinctoria:* 30-50 cm (12-38 ins); *Spartium junceum:* 3-4 cm (10-13 ft).
SOIL TYPE Friable, well drained, lime-free.
MOISTURE Watering is not necessary.
POSITION Full sun.
CLIMATE Temperate-Mediterranean conditions. The spartium (Spanish broom) is naturalized in California and the genista (dyer's greenweed) is naturalized in eastern North America.
PROPAGATION By cuttings in summer. By seed in spring.
TRANSPLANTING TIME Autumn-spring. The adult plants do not like being transplanted.
FLOWERING TIME Late spring to early summer. The flowers are golden-yellow and fragrant.
USES In shrub borders and the genista to cover slopes. Also as cut flowers. *G. tinctoria* has been a source of dyes.
CUTTING BACK The branches of young plants should be shortened after flowering to encourage them to bush out. Older plants can be thinned out as necessary to retain a good open shape.
PESTS Young plants are easy prey for caterpillars and snails.
DISEASES Mildew, rust, viruses.

Tulip
Tulipa sylvestris (1)
Tulipa sp. (2)

FAMILY *Liliaceae*.
PLACE OF ORIGIN Turkey, Europe, central Asia and the Middle East.
TYPE OF PLANT Herbaceous, bulbous perennials, with light or silvery green, lance-head-shaped leaves, which grow upwards.
HEIGHT 10-60 cm (4-24 ins).
SOIL TYPE Well drained, average garden soil that is slightly acid to slightly alkaline.
MOISTURE Abundant watering only after flowering while leaves are ripening and before bulbs become dormant.
POSITION Sunny or semi-shaded.
CLIMATE Temperate.
PROPAGATION Separation of the bulbs, after the foliage has died, in early summer to autumn. Also from seeds of species – but seeds of hybrids may not resemble their parents and under home-garden conditions, probably will not bloom for three or four years.
TRANSPLANTING TIME Summer to autumn when bulbs are dormant. New bulbs from dealers are available only in autumn.
FLOWERING TIME Early to late spring, according to species and offspring. *T. sylvestris*, yellow flowers, in mid to late spring.
USES The many species and some of their varieties in rock gardens; the usually taller, more formal modern tulips massed in beds, especially in parks and public places, in drifts in flower borders and in front of shrubs. Also forced in pots for winter-to-early-spring flowers in greenhouses and among other house plants. In outdoor gardens, annuals usually follow the tulips as their bulbs' foliage dies down after flowering.
PESTS Snails and rabbits may chew on emerging foliage. Mice delight in eating the bulbs.
DISEASES Grey mould and bulb rot.

Periwinkle
Vinca major (1)
Vinca minor (2)

FAMILY *Apocynaceae*.
PLACE OF ORIGIN Europe.
TYPE OF PLANT Herbaceous perennial or subshrub, evergreen, with leathery eliptical leaves; the older stems are prostrate and woody, with a tendency to make roots. *V. minor* also known as running myrtle.
HEIGHT 15-30 cm (6-12 ins).
SOIL TYPE Tolerant of varying types but prefer humus-rich, friable conditions.
MOISTURE Regular watering in really dry spells.
POSITION Semi-shade to full shade.
CLIMATE *V. minor* is very hardy; *V. major* is not winter-hardy in the North.
PROPAGATION By stolons, or digging mats or "sods" in spring or autumn.
TRANSPLANTING TIME The plants can be divided at any time in the South, providing the ground is not too cold and the new plants are planted immediately. In the North, early spring or autumn are usual times.
FLOWERING TIME Lilac-coloured or light blue flowers in spring.
USES As ground-cover for shrubberies and in lieu of grass in shady places, on banks, and around terraces; *V. major* looks very attractive in summer hanging down from pots or hanging baskets or window boxes, its main use in the North.
PESTS Aphids.
DISEASES *V. major* is somewhat prone to grey mould and rust.

Violet
Viola odorata

FAMILY *Violaceae*.
PLACE OF ORIGIN Asia, Mediterranean basin.
TYPE OF PLANT Herbaceous perennial, rhizomatous with heart-shaped leaves. Its stems often produce stolons. The common name for *V. odorata* is sweet violet.
HEIGHT 10-15 cm (4-6 ins).
SOIL TYPE Fertile, well drained, moist soil.
MOISTURE Frequent watering, especially when grown in dry places.
POSITION Sunny or slightly shaded, sheltered.
CLIMATE Temperate.
PROPAGATION By seed (the plants self-sow) and separation of the new little plants from the main stems in early summer or autumn.
TRANSPLANTING TIME Autumn or early spring.
FLOWERING TIME Late winter to spring, depending on climate. These sweetly scented flowers are, of course, violet in colour but there are varieties which have white, pink, purple, mauve and also double flowers.
USES In borders, rock gardens, naturalized in woodlands and in pots in greenhouses.
PESTS Aphids

Pansy
Viola tricolor (1)
Viola wittrockiana (2)

FAMILY *Violaceae*.
PLACE OF ORIGIN Europe.
TYPE OF PLANT Shortlived herbaceous perennial, usually grown as a biennial. It has a branched stem with elongated, light green leaves. Johnny-jump-up is *V. tricolor*. By crossing *V. tricolor* with related species a large number of varieties and hybrids has been obtained, which are comprehensively known as the pansy – *V.* x *wittrockiana*.
HEIGHT 5-20 cm (2-8 ins), according to the variety.
SOIL TYPE Fertile, well drained, preferably slightly acid.
MOISTURE Regular watering.
POSITION Sunny or semi-shaded.
CLIMATE Temperate-cool.
PROPAGATION By seed from summer to early autumn, depending upon the climate. Johnny-jump-up will self-sow freely.
TRANSPLANTING TIME Spring or autumn.
FLOWERING TIME Mostly spring – or until stopped by hot, humid weather. The flowers have a flat corolla or "face" in colours ranging through white to yellow, violet, light blue and crimson; many have two colours or are variegated.
USES In borders and rock gardens; pansies are also suitable for growing in pots on balconies and in window-boxes, but rarely survive hot summers.
CUTTING BACK Removing fading flowers is advisable to prolong the flowering period.
PESTS Red spider mites and nematodes in some regions.
DISEASES Grey mould, mildew, root rot.

Mistletoe
Viscum album

FAMILY *Loranthaceae*.
PLACE OF ORIGIN Europe, northern Asia.
TYPE OF PLANT Shrub, globous, semi-parasitical; its branches are green and its stiff evergreen leaves are grouped in pairs. It lives on trees, such as apple, silver fir, spruce, poplar, Scotch pine, mountain ash and others.
HEIGHT 50-100 cm (20-40 ins).
POSITION Facing north.
PROPAGATION By seed in autumn-spring, by insertion into cracks in the bark of the host trees.
FLOWERING TIME Late winter to spring. The insignificant greenish-yellow male and female flowers form on separate plants, the white berries forming on female plants.
USES The branches are cut for end-of-year festivities.

Wisteria
Wisteria sinensis

FAMILY *Leguminosae*.
PLACE OF ORIGIN China for *W. sinensis*; other species from Japan and eastern United States.
TYPE OF PLANT Woody shrub, climber, twining; its leaves are compound with an irregular number of leaflets (7-13) arranged in pairs on opposite sides of the leaf stem and with a terminal leaflet. Its long thin, trailing shoots entwine themselves tightly around any available supports.
HEIGHT This can vary from 10-20 m (33-66 ft.)
SOIL TYPE Preferably humus-rich, moist and deep but not too limy.
POSITION Sunny or partially shaded; a sheltered position in very cold climates.
CLIMATE Temperate. It grows well everywhere, but is not as hardy as the Japanese wisteria (*W. floribunda*).
PROPAGATION Preferably by layering starting in spring. By cuttings in summer.
TRANSPLANTING TIME Early spring or autumn. There must always be plenty of room for the roots to spread out.
FLOWERING TIME Late spring. The flowers are borne in drooping trusses; they are only slightly fragrant and usually lilac-blue in colour; the "Jako" and "Alba" varieties have white flowers and are especially fragrant.
USES As a climber on pergolas, trellises, walls, but should be kept from shingled houses. If pruned correctly, it can also be made to grow like a small tree (called a standard). Wisteria can be grown in large pots or tubs on terraces, patios. But this will restrict its growth, of course.
CUTTING BACK This is done twice: in early summer, the new side branches should be cut back to 6 buds and, in early spring, these can be shortened again by another 3 buds.
PESTS Aphids, red spider mites.
DISEASES Chlorosis if the soil is too alkaline.

Calla lily
Zantedeschia aethiopica

FAMILY *Araceae*.
PLACE OF ORIGIN South Africa.
TYPE OF PLANT Tender, herbaceous perennial, rhizomatous, with glossy, arrow shaped leaves on long leaf-stalks.
HEIGHT 50-100 cm (20-40 ins).
SOIL TYPE Damp garden soil, preferably at the edge of a pool or lake and submerged in water to a depth of 10-30 cm (4-12 ins) in mild frost-free regions. Elsewhere in pots.
MOISTURE Abundant watering from the appearance of the shoots until the end of the flowering period. In the case of plants in pots, watering should be decreased gradually and stopped altogether when the leaves have dried.
POSITION Shade or semi-shade.
CLIMATE Temperate-mild. In northern areas, the plants should be allowed to go dormant and over-wintered in a frost-free area until spring.
PROPAGATION By division of the rhizomes in the spring or autumn.
TRANSPLANTING TIME Early spring; in the North, rhizomes are usually potted indoors in early spring and brought outdoors when weather has warmed.
FLOWERING TIME Late spring to summer. The flowers consist of a spike of yellow flowers (spadix) enclosed in a white bract (spathe) supported on a smooth, erect stem.
USES To decorate the edges of pools, fountain basins, terraces in the open ground or in pots. Also as cut flowers.
DISEASES Root rot and leaf spot.

Zinnia
Zinnia hybrids

FAMILY *Compositae*.
PLACE OF ORIGIN Mexico, Chile, southwestern United States of America.
TYPE OF PLANT Herbaceous annual or perennial, with an erect habit and rough, dark green, oval leaves. Usually grown as an annual.
HEIGHT 15-80 cm (6-32 ins).
SOIL TYPE Any well drained average garden soil.
MOISTURE Regular watering during drought.
POSITION Sunny.
CLIMATE Temperate.
PROPAGATION By seed in flats indoors about three weeks before weather outdoors has warmed. Or sow outdoors when frosts end.
TRANSPLANTING TIME Spring.
FLOWERING TIME Summer-autumn. The flowers can be single, double or semi-double in various shades of red, pink, yellow, lavender, orange or white.
USES In flowerbeds, borders and in pots. Useful as cut flowers.
CUTTING BACK The tops should be pinched out of the young plants to encourage branching and, thus, more flowers. Remove fading flowers before seeds form.
PESTS Stalk borer and Japanese beetle.
DISEASES Mildew.

Select bibliography

Boland, B. *Gardener's Magic*, The Bodley Head, London
Boland, M. and Boland, B. *Old Wives' Lore for Gardeners*, The Bodley Head, London
Bourne, E. and Baker, A. *Heritage of Flowers*, Putnam Sons, New York
Bryan, J. E. and Castle, C. *The Edible Ornamental Garden*, Pitman Ltd., London
de Bray, L. *Fantastic Garlands*, Blandford Press, Poole
Forte, V. *Noi e le Piante*, Edagricole, Bologna
Grande Enciclopedia del Giardinaggio, Curcio Editore, Rome
Gubernatis, A. de *La Mythologie des Plantes*, Arche, Milan
Kaiti, L. *Piante e Profumi Magici*, Editrice Atanor, Rome
Mercatante, A. *The Magic Garden*, Harper and Row, New York
Pickston, M. *The Language of Flowers*, Michael Joseph Ltd., London
Pizzetti, I. and Cocker, H. *Il Libro dei Fiori*, Garzanti, Milan
Powell, C. *The Meaning of Flowers*, Shambhala Publications Inc., Boulder, Colorado
Rodway, A. and Reddy, M. *A Literary Herbal*, Hutchinson, London
Salvy, C. *Linguaggio dei Fiori*, Edizioni Corticelli, Milan
Seymour, J. *Gardener's Delight*, Michael Joseph Ltd., London
Skargon, Y. *Handful of Flowers*, Adam & Charles Black, London

INDEX